To Rev. E. Rowlan

With every good wish for
1961

From - H. E. Heathcote.

THE PARISH SEEKS THE WAY

THE PARISH SEEKS THE WAY

A strategy for a working-class parish

BY THE REV.

MICHAEL HOCKING

Vicar of St. Ambrose's, East Bristol

LONDON

A. R. MOWBRAY & Co. LIMITED

© *A. R. Mowbray & Co. Limited, 1960*

First published in 1960

PRINTED IN GREAT BRITAIN BY
A. R. MOWBRAY & CO. LIMITED IN THE CITY OF OXFORD
063

FOREWORD

IN these days, when there is much talk about the need for the Church 'to be the Church,' it is always refreshing to find a parish in which the Church actually is the Church—a living fellowship. I believe St. Ambrose, Bristol, is such a church. In these days, too, when so much is talked about 'biblical theology,' it is encouraging to find a church putting theology into practice and going ahead on lines which are both scriptural and at the same time traditional in the best possible sense of that thrilling word. In St. Ambrose, Bristol, biblical theology has been 'earthed' in an Anglican expression of church life which is both catholic and reformed.

I count it, therefore, a privilege to write a foreword to this book—and for two special reasons:

(1) I have visited and worked for a short time in this parish. I know what Michael Hocking is talking about. What he says is true.

(2) This is an ordinary working-class parish. As far as I could judge, apart from a very good church hall next to the church, it has no special assets. What Michael Hocking has done in this parish seems to me to be what others could do elsewhere. It has been essentially an adventure in team work, but the success of the team has not been made possible by any special stunt or spectacular personality, although the vicar has given a decisive lead. Honest to goodness 'blood and sweat and tears,' much prayer, real authority and discipline, and a vicarage that is a Christian home have been among its secrets.

J. E. FISON

GREAT ST. MARY'S VICARAGE
CAMBRIDGE

CONTENTS

CONTENTS

INTRODUCTION

I AM one of those people who greatly enjoy reading about other parishes. I find it absorbingly interesting to find out what is being done elsewhere, what new experiments are being tried out, what general strategy is bringing good results. The trouble is that most of the available accounts deal with well-staffed parishes with great traditions or parishes with vast populations or high-powered incumbents of outstanding ability. I have a story to tell of a small parish. It has no great traditions. It has a population of less than six thousand. No well-known people live here. It is working class, and proud of it.

I am now in my seventh year, having moved here rather reluctantly from one of the most attractive of all Cornish parishes, a parish where one could easily have sunk into a comfortable rut. My heart sank when I saw for the first time the streets surrounding the parish church of St. Ambrose, East Bristol. The contrast with the glories of Mount's Bay that I could see from my study window and the Cornish cliffs and moors in my parish could not have been more marked, and I began to think of all the reasons why I could not possibly move. But my first view of the interior of the church made me hesitate. It is a magnificent building, completed in 1913, and planned on the grand scale. I found there were two church halls, ample vestries and committee rooms, a good modern vicarage and garden, and a clergy house containing two flats, all built on one splendid site overlooking a park.

The traditions of the parish were, I was told, Conservative Evangelical, but the Parochial Church Council had exercised their statutory right, and had asked for a change of tradition and the appointment of a Central Churchman. Certainly the place was rather dead. Congregations averaged about twenty communicants at 8 a.m., twenty-five or so at 11 a.m. Mattins (mostly elderly), and sixty or seventy at Evensong. They were clearly keen and devoted and loved their church for the place was spotless, and the collections, amounting to about £7 a Sunday, were quite good for such small numbers. Although the church was always short of money, generous support was given to the Church Missionary Society. The choir and ringers were good, but the only flourishing church organization appeared to be the Mothers' Union.

There were several small factories in the parish, but most of the men worked in the bigger factories elsewhere. There were six schools catering for children of all ages from all over Bristol. Many of the streets had the front doors opening on to the pavement, and there were also a number of owner-occupied houses built between the wars with trim gardens front and rear and several hundred pre-fabs.

I came home to talk it over with my wife, and to think and pray about this unsought and disturbing challenge, and to talk it over with people whose opinions I valued. My wife came to have a look—and was as shaken as I was. However, gradually we became convinced that it was right to accept. She decided that she could manage the house without domestic help if some fairly extensive alterations could be done. The diocesan authorities were more than helpful, and all other difficulties were swept away one by one.

I came here in 1954 full of ideas, and everything was in my favour for carrying them out. The place was far from alive, and the people wanted, indeed had asked for, drastic changes. They longed to see their church occupying the place they felt it ought to occupy, they wanted newcomers to join and young people to come in and conversions to take place. Most were outward looking and willing to consider almost anything. How do I know that? I thought in ordinary fairness that before accepting I ought to meet the Parochial Church Council and lay before them the general strategy that I meant to pursue.

I explained to them what Central Churchmanship really meant and what immediate changes were proposed, and why, and I undertook not to do anything really important without taking them fully into my confidence. They pledged their wholehearted support.

This book tells the story of those changes and the results. I hope it will not seem too disconnected, but it will be appreciated that it has been written under difficulties. A town vicarage is not the ideal place for that quiet, undisturbed concentration that I imagine writers usually enjoy. This book has been written amid the normal turmoil we take for granted, with telephone and doorbell ringing, and visitors calling and all sorts of matters distracting one's chain of thought. That is the way we like it. But I fear that the effects will be apparent.

Then there is the family. My children have left me alone for unusually long periods, but sometimes there has been a lapse and on one occasion my younger son was assembling his fishing gear, including bait, and I looked up to see seven horrible fat maggots advancing purposefully across my desk, an occupational hazard for which I was not prepared. Lapses of this sort have been few. But I defy anybody to remain calm and collected in the face of them.

And I must apologize for the excessive use of the word 'I.' It has proved impossible to avoid using it time and again, for I must take the ultimate responsibility for all that has been planned and carried out. But it has been a team effort. I gladly pay tribute to the outstanding work of Richard Easton, my first assistant curate, who joined me three months after my arrival and stayed for three and a half years. He and I talked out almost everything at length, and his enthusiasm and devotion were a constant inspiration. His successor, Harvey Pentreath, like myself a Cornishman, is quite outstanding and full of ideas. My wife has made the running of the home and the care of the family her first job, but she helps in countless ways, doing things that a mere man could never do, and never

asking questions about the confidential matters that come
along so frequently.

The former Bishop of Bristol, Dr. Cockin, who was
consulted about everything important, was more than
helpful, and his great experience and wisdom were made
freely available. He could so easily have cautiously dis-
couraged this and firmly forbidden that, but this was not
his way; nor is it that of his successor, Dr. Tomkins, who,
on his first visit to this parish, celebrated at the Family
Communion and earned the gratitude of us all by doing
everything in the exact way that we always do it.

My churchwardens, P.C.C. members, and leaders of
organizations have always accepted my leadership and
worked loyally and well. Although they have not always
agreed with me—usually rightly—they have done all
that has been asked of them; and this, as will be seen,
has not been inconsiderable.

The news columns of the newspapers are usually read
before leading articles, and you cannot get a balanced
view of what is happening without reading both. There
are plenty of books of the leading article type available,
but those containing news stories are in short supply,
and that is why this book has been written. The news is
not sensational. It discloses the strategy adopted in one
particular parish. We are seeking the Way, using that
word in its New Testament sense, and this book tells the
story of that search and the results so far. My hope is
that other parish priests may find time to tell their news
stories too, and thus help us all.

MICHAEL HOCKING

PART ONE
THE OVERALL STRATEGY

CHAPTER ONE

BACK TO THE NEW TESTAMENT

THINGS have certainly happened here, and visiting preachers have expressed surprise that in such a parish so much should have happened so quickly. Why is it that we should expect so little from working-class parishes? Why is it that so often services are dreary and dull and badly attended?

There are thousands of parishes rather like mine in many respects, and in all too many of them the incumbents have got a bit depressed by the absence of response. They work for long hours, hours that would make a good trade unionist shudder. I believe that in lots of parishes such as this things could happen, given a few basic principles.

The first of these is that the incumbent really wants things to happen, and is prepared to put the glorifying of God's name and the enlargement of His kingdom (as the ordinal puts it) before narrow sectional interests. The rather colourless old-fashioned 11 a.m. Sung Mattins of the Conservative Evangelicals on the one hand, and the equally old-fashioned very elaborate 11 a.m. Sung Mass of the Anglo-Catholics, with Western use and all the rest of it, on the other, simply will not do in a working-class parish. If people want extreme simplicity they will tend to go to the Gospel Halls that abound in such districts. If they want all the elaborations they will probably go to the Roman church where they will find greater numbers of like-minded people. It is Central Churchmanship, positive and definite as I hope to show later on, that our folk really understand and want.

The second basic principle is that the Parish Communion must be the central service, with everything leading up to it and away from it. This is the very heart and core of the whole parish strategy that must be worked out and adhered to, and I shall have a lot to say about this farther on. Other features of this parish strategy include making the fullest use of the faithful laity, laying tremendous stress on the vital importance of Holy Baptism and Confirmation, and using the opportunities for evangelism that the Occasional Offices provide. Evangelism is the key word. We are not private chaplains. We are missionary leaders, and much of our work consists of making opportunities for leading our people to God.

This is no new strategy; on the contary, it is surely basic New Testament. How we long for things to happen now as they certainly happened then! J. B. Phillips, who has done such magnificent work in translating the New Testament into modern speech, catches the wonder and the glory of those stirring days when he says:

The fresh air of Heaven blows gustily through these pages, and the sense that ordinary human life is continually open to the Spirit of God is very marked. There is not yet a dead hand of tradition; there is no over-organization to stifle initiative; there is neither security nor complacency to destroy sensitivity to the living God. The early Church lived dangerously, but never before has such a handful of people exerted such widespread influence. There is courage to match the vision; there is a flexible willingness to match the divine leadership. And there is that unshakeable certainty against which persecution, imprisonment and death prove quite powerless. To put it shortly and in the common phrase, the lasting excitement that follows the reading of this book is this: THE THING WORKS! (*New Testament Christianity*, p. 15).

J. B. Phillips writes about the Acts of the Apostles. Surely it is becoming increasingly clear that our own Church of England, firmly based on the Bible, is turning back to those early days and putting first the things which the early followers of Jesus put first. The longer I remain a parish priest the more convinced I am that the New Testament points the way for our parish strategy. Already in the Acts the weekly Breaking of Bread has become the centre, the focal point. Holy Baptism is clearly of tremendous importance and significance and theologians such as Lampe have shown us clearly that it is all wrong to push it quietly into the background as a matter of no interest except to the parents or individuals concerned. It is a great Gospel sacrament conferring the gift of the Holy Spirit, and not a mere preliminary, a hole-in-the-corner formality that pales into comparative insignificance when compared with Confirmation. Confirmation is surely of equal but not greater importance. Hebrews 6 [2] tells us clearly that baptism and the laying on of hands are among the first principles of Christ, and thus naturally the annual Confirmation and the Public Baptisms must be regarded as some of the greatest occasions of the whole year.

The place of the laity is defined in ringing terms in 1 Peter 2:

Ye also, as living stones, are built up a spiritual house, to be a holy priesthood, to offer up spiritual sacrifices, acceptable to God through Jesus Christ. . . . Ye are an elect race, a royal priesthood, a holy nation, a people for God's own possession, that ye may show forth the excellencies of Him who called you out of darkness into His marvellous light: which in time past were no people, but now are the people of God: which had not obtained mercy, but now have obtained mercy.

In every parish there is a small nucleus of faithful laity who are longing to be trusted and trained and used, and I am quite clear that no parish can be run properly without their wholehearted co-operation and support. I remember at one C.E.M.S. meeting I was asked these questions. 'Vicar, is it correct that you and you alone have the authority to alter the times of service, to decide which services shall be choral and which not, and whether a sermon shall be preached?' 'Do you decide who can play the organ, what can be played, and when?' 'Have you the authority to appoint and dismiss assistant curates, organists, caretakers, and all other paid members of the staff?' 'Is it your prerogative to decide what sort of social functions shall be held in the parish, and when?' After a number of such questions one member said: 'It seems to me that the vicar can turn the whole place upside down if he wants to.' And so he can—but he is a fool if he does! When the incumbent and his people are at loggerheads, nothing useful can be achieved, but in partnership nothing is impossible.

And surely 'fellowship' is another of the great New Testament words. It suggests participation and sharing; and it suggests companionship, hospitality, and friendliness. Tertullian tells us that the comment of the pagan world when they saw the Christians in their midst was quite simply, 'See how these Christians love one another.' We cannot be content with any lesser standard. This is simply another basic principle, and I must admit, rather sadly, that it is just about the hardest of the lot to get across in a working-class parish.

My people have heard a lot about being the family, behaving like a family, making new members of the family. This consciousness breathes through passage after passage in the New Testament and carried all before it, and we simply must allow nothing to mar it to-day.

Expectancy is found in the New Testament, most of all in the Acts of the Apostles. The disciples expected something great and wonderful to happen when they waited in the upper room at Pentecost, and they went on expecting that through them the Holy Spirit would perform mighty acts. I had something to say about expecting great things, about being used by the Holy Spirit, in my Cornish parish magazine ten years ago, and I would like to say it again here:

Unhappily, conversion is taken for granted where it does not exist. How can you tell it does not exist? By spiritual deadness and inertia in so many churches, churches where nothing ever happens, churches where few demands are made, where people are not expected to come if it is too wet or too cold or too hot or too dry, churches where services and meetings are expected to take second place to things like weeding the garden or cleaning the car, churches where enthusiasm and fellowship and witness are neither understood nor desired. Our non-converted worshippers seem almost to apologize for their religion at times, as though they were somehow subnormal and the people who never worship anywhere the normal ones.

Contrast this with the wonderful picture of the converted few painted in the opening chapters of the Acts of the Apostles. Their joy and enthusiasm were infectious. They so clearly had something which the others lacked and which others soon began to want.

They proclaimed what that something was to all who would listen, so that new people were constantly coming into the fellowship. They worshipped together, studied together, shared a common meal in each other's houses. Their worship led to witness, that is, they told other people just what their Risen Lord meant to them, and what He would mean to anybody who accepted Him as master and friend. They offered to strangers first friendship and then salvation. Their wonderful faith overcame shyness and diffidence, and in time it overcame hostility and persecution and death.

We desperately need a return of this spirit of triumph. How is it to be achieved? If there is ever to be a revival of religion here or anywhere else it will not be by great mass meetings addressed by star speakers. It is far more likely that it will be by ordinary everyday intercourse between converted Christians and those at present outside the churches, and the movement may well start by quiet conversations on the land or in factory, office or workshop. The really serious thing to-day is that most of our worshippers have never even tried to lead anybody to Christ, would not know how to start such a conversation, do not believe that God could and would use them if they would allow themselves to be used.

Looking back at that article I do not think I want to change any of it. It simply stresses the need to return to the New Testament for a basic strategy that really works now as it did then, and I reiterated the same plea in more detailed terms in my New Year letter in the January 1958 parish magazine:

There is an immense amount to be done this year, and in general our policy remains quite simply 'Back to the New Testament.' The longer I remain a parish priest the more convinced I am that the New Testament must remain our standard and our authority and the more certain I am that the Acts of the Apostles points the way. THEY walked with our Lord and were taught by Him. They put into practice what He said. Down the centuries all sorts of additions and sub-tractions have been made. The one undivided Church split into many parts and much of supreme value has been lost. We can thank God that our own Church of England, Catholic and Reformed, has tried and is still trying to stress the things that were stressed in the earliest days, and we believe our Church is nearest of all to the clear teaching we find there. Acts 2^{42} sums up the practice of the first generation of Christians, and here is a summary based upon it of what we want to do here this year.

THEY attached great importance to the teaching of the Apostles. So must we. Doctrine is not a dull subject, and I believe that people love to hear the great Christian doctrines explained in such a way that they can themselves explain these things to others. There will be more teaching sermons. If you find them dull and heavy, for goodness' sake say so. No parson ever minds friendly and constructive criticism, a different matter entirely from the voicing of petty grievances. We shall try to preach the Gospel in its fullness as it was and as it will always be, and we shall try to apply it to modern life and to modern problems. We want well-instructed Ambrosians who really know the facts, but sermons alone can never achieve this. It can never be unless people read their Bibles daily as well.

THEY attached great importance to fellowship. So must we. Are we a friendly church? Can I absolutely guarantee that newcomers who join our fellowship will really be welcomed, that people will talk to them and make them feel members of our family? The family gathering after Family Communion is the best chance of all and the six public baptisms in 1958 will provide others. An unfriendly, unsociable Christian is a contradiction in terms. It was this fellowship in the early Church that so impressed the pagan world, and it is no less important to-day.

THEY attached great importance to the Breaking of Bread. So must we. I imagine all Ambrosians regard our beautiful and inspiring Family Communion as clearly our focal point—and about half our members come every Sunday. In the New Testament it seems clear that every member was present every Sunday, and if they were prevented from coming by sickness the sacred elements were taken to them immediately after the service. We will gladly do this if anybody will send a message the night before. This year let's try to get all our members, including of course the children, to make every Sunday a normal obligation. If even one member is absent the service is spoiled to some extent.

THEY attached great importance to prayers. So must we. The Revised Version makes it read 'The Prayers' and this suggests services other than Holy Communion. I want to see Evensong livened up this year, with more present, and better singing and greater enthusiasm.

The Acts of the Apostles shows us what can happen in the sort of atmosphere in which the Holy Spirit can work. Given that atmosphere, things can and do happen, but before describing some of those things I want to say something about two expressions that I have used but not defined, 'working class' and 'Central Churchmanship.'

CHAPTER TWO

WORKING CLASS AND CENTRAL CHURCHMANSHIP

IT is sometimes said that in these democratic days the term 'working class' is out of date. As we move steadily towards the classless society that may be one of the end products of the welfare state, it is true that the old distinctions of upper, middle, and working class are ceasing to be as rigid as they used to be in, for instance, the time of Dickens. It was Mr. Jingle who described to Mr. Tupman the guests at the Rochester Charity Ball thus: 'Dockyard people of upper rank don't know dockyard people of lower rank—dockyard people of lower rank don't know small gentry—small gentry don't know tradespeople—commissioner don't know anybody.' Things have changed since the publication of *Pickwick Papers*, and are still changing, but it remains a fact that there are still a great many working-class parishes where the parishioners are conscious of it and proud of it, and I am reminded here time and again that 'we are a working-class parish, vicar.'

I took up with my elders (a body of senior churchmen whose composition and function are described farther on) their frequent use of this term, and posed to them these questions:

(1) What do you mean by 'working class'?
(2) Is it a term to be proud of, or is it in any sense derogatory?
(3) Is it the ambition of working-class folk to move into the middle class?

After a careful discussion they came unanimously to these conclusions:

(1) The term 'working class' describes those who work hardest with their hands and do the greater part of the real work upon which our country depends.

(2) It is a term to be proud of, unlike 'lower class' which has snobbish associations, and is thus thoroughly offensive.

(3) Working-class folk have no ambition to transfer to the middle class whether they go up in the world or not. But there are some exceptions to this, and they do not have a high opinion of those who tend to look down on their former associates.

Working-class churchmen are conscious of the fact that they serve a Master who once worked with His hands and thus hallowed manual work for all time. It is in the light of these comments that I have not hesitated to give this book its sub-title.

The men include those who, generally speaking, are employees rather than employers. They are the members of the trades unions. They may be skilled tradesmen, semi-skilled workmen, or unskilled labourers. They earn anything from £8 to £20 a week or more, with overtime including Sunday work at double rates. The married women often work full time or part time, and bring in perhaps £3–£7 a week in addition. They vote pretty solidly for the Labour candidate in local or parliamentary elections, although not so solidly as they used to do in less prosperous days. They are still suspicious of the boss, of management generally, of the Tory party, and, to a much lesser degree, of the Church of England.

One great feature of the working class is solidarity and loyalty to fellow members, and this may sometimes take a peculiar form. For instance, I once saw a girl on a parish outing neatly putting her empty sweet bag and banana skin on the floor of the bus under her seat, only to be loudly rebuked by her mother: 'Winnie, how often have I got to tell you not to do that? Don't you know that somebody has got to clean out this bus to-morrow morning? Throw your rubbish out of the window, then nobody will have to clear it up!' At best this loyalty, this consideration for fellow workers, can be a splendid thing, and it is the usual practice when a man is sick and on reduced money for his workmates to put something into the kitty when they receive their weekly pay packets, and thus make up the deficit. You see it at its worst when somebody refuses to obey a strike call or refuses to join the union or in some way strikes an independent line. The sending to Coventry and other vicious actions that result are not edifying, but they are the seemingly inevitable result of anything that looks like breaking this solidarity.

The distinctive sin is materialism, the modern version of the old deadly sin of gluttony. Gluttony of the old kind may be out. Parson Woodford tells us in his diary, written in 1784, that 'We had a very genteel Dinner, Soals and Lobster Sauce, Spring Chicken boiled and a Tongue, a Piece of rost Beef, Soup, a Fillet of Veal rosted with Morells and Trufles, and Pigeon Pie for the first Course—Sweetbreads, a green Goose and Peas, Apricot Pye, Cheese-cakes, Stewed Mushrooms and Trifle,' and we can breathe a sigh of relief that such excesses are no longer with us. The real gluttony lies not in food but in things. All the emphasis now in working-class England is on the standard of living, and the news-paper that prophesies that this standard will double in twenty-five years can be sure of a vast circulation. The money that comes in goes out. Everybody wants all the latest appliances, first the modern semi-detached house, then a radio-gramophone, a television set, a vacuum cleaner, a washing machine, and so on in endless pro-fusion. I can take you to one house where there is a 21in. television set in the front room and a 17in. set in the back room. And you do not need to save up for these things. There is almost nothing that cannot be bought on hire purchase, and the thoroughly bad thing in this frantic endeavour to keep up with the neighbours is that the more you have the more you want. I shall have some more to say later on about the effects of working incredible hours, and wives leaving their children to come home to an empty house, all for the sole purpose of getting more and more of the latest consumer goods.

It is becoming increasingly clear that the whole future of the country is in their hands. To them the sales talk must be addressed. More vital still, production is in their hands. We must export manufactured goods if we are to survive. They must be of superb quality and sold at competitive prices, and it is the skill and restraint of the working classes that can make both possible. Equally, skill can become obsolete and old traditions can die. Wage demands can be pressed until production costs make sales impossible. Strikes can paralyse the whole country. Never was it more vital that the working-class youngsters who pour out from our state schools should have high ideals, should see that work is something to be done as in the sight of God, should feel a sense of responsibility for the well-being of the whole realm, and ultimately of the whole world. They should know where they come from, what they are here for, and where they are going. In short, they want the knowledge and convictions that come from God, and are nurtured by membership of the Church.

There are signs that the Church of England is aware of the challenge and opportunity of the present time. The remark of Lord Melbourne after hearing a certain sermon, that 'things have come to a pretty pass when religion is allowed to invade the sphere of private life,' indicates how far we have moved in the past hundred years. The efforts to bring religion into the factories and workshops at all levels are described in Bishop Wickham's *Church and People in an Industrial City*, surely one of the most exciting books of recent years, and one that would have rejoiced the heart of Archbishop Temple. This Sheffield experiment is being carried out in other industrial centres, and is surely bound to help to bridge the gap between the working classes and the Church. But we are bound to ask ourselves this question—Is our parochial machinery being geared to meet the needs of working-class folk? Are we leaving these industrial chaplains suspended in mid-air? Are we still a middle-class Church?

We certainly used to be. For generations this has been so. The most flourishing churches tended to be located in pleasant suburban districts, and they were the best attended, had the biggest collections, paid the highest quotas, and kept the missionary societies going. Working-class churches tended to be more sparsely attended. Of course there used to be great poverty to contend with. Wonderful work was done by truly great people, but it was material bread rather than the spiritual kind that people felt they needed most, and they just stayed away. Bishop Winnington-Ingram sent many of us to East End parishes in London 'to win our spurs' as he put it. In fact, much of our work was of the kind that social workers are now trained to do. Our needy parishioners were not conspicuous by their presence on Sunday mornings, although many would come on Sunday evenings if the service was bright and lively.

We did not really expect them to come on Sunday mornings. We had our 8 a.m. Holy Communion. Did we really expect men who had to be up at 6 a.m. all the rest of the week to come? We had our 11 a.m. Mattins, a service that achieved centrality by an accident of history, and that was really intended for the middle and upper classes who had servants to cook for them. Did we really expect those who did come to be transported with enthusiasm by the stately language of the seventeenth century? Some famous East End parishes had High Mass at the same hour, but how many ordinary working-class men were present Sunday by Sunday?

We did not get, nor did we expect to get, great numbers of ordinary working-class men to attend our traditional services. The Gospel halls, the Salvation Army, the Church Army, the Roman Catholic Church—these all seemed to achieve a good deal more than we did. At

Diocesan Conferences we bewailed the fact that somehow the Church of England did not make much appeal to the working classes, and we continued to look for the bulk of our support to the middle classes from which our ordinands were largely drawn.

We still do, of course. We are still largely a middle-class Church. But there is one significant difference that must be noted, and this is that the Church of England is beginning to make a greater appeal to the working classes; greater, for instance, than that made by Nonconformity.

We are beginning to see that it is in the working-class parishes that we have at the present time our greatest opportunity. The old hostilities are dying away and for various reasons, one of which is, surely, the good work being put in by the industrial chaplains, the men are beginning to come in. At present it is only a trickle, but it is enough to indicate that there is a hunger for spiritual bread, a faith by which to live, an ideology. People are ready at least to give the Church a hearing, and parishes which have a clear and definite strategy are beginning to produce results.

I believe this strategy should be based on Central Churchmanship convictions. My people asked for it after years of Conservative Evangelicalism, and they are not alone in wanting it. It is something that they can understand and appreciate because it is positive and constructive.

This point needs amplifying. Central Churchmanship is popularly supposed to be a dim grey affair that involves caution and sitting on the fence and a general refusal to make up one's mind. Perhaps it used to be. When there were many more extremists than there are now, perhaps there were numbers of so-called Central Churchmen who were just not able to make up their minds where they stood, and thus contented themselves with a long list of things they did not believe in, and were hazy and uncertain about the rest. Perhaps there were such people, but if so I met very few of them. Central

Churchmen are people with a positive faith who, after carefully examining the claims of the extremists, try to select the best and retain the historically true and pastorally valuable and avoid like the plague the old arid deserts of unedifying controversy.

This is what we have tried to do here. We have retained or introduced a number of things that the Evangelicals have always considered to be of vital importance. They have always insisted on the need for conversion and personal religion and the vital necessity for decision and acceptance of the claims of Christ. So do we. Sermons, confirmation classes, magazine articles, interviews, sick visits, all provide opportunities for doing just this, and we gladly accept them.

The Bible has always been the book of books, the very word of God, to the Evangelicals—and so it is to us. The ministry of the Word is vitally important, and we urge our people to come to church on Sunday evenings as well as mornings, because it is there that there is always a lesson from the Old Testament, and it is there that more time can be spent in preaching and expounding. Our people are urged to take the Bible Reading Fellowship or Scripture Union notes, and between thirty and forty do, but more than this read the Bible daily. Some prefer to do without the notes. We have a weekly Bible study group, when we go through one of the books chapter by chapter, and all present are invited to ask questions or make comments.

The prayer meeting is thought to be old-fashioned nowadays, but this was always a great feature of Evangelical churches and it is surely sound New Testament practice. We have had one here ever since my induction, and although the attendance rarely exceeds a dozen or so, yet I believe it to be of very great value. Anybody present offers extempore prayer, and I find the simply expressed prayers that are not perhaps phrased in faultless English, but which come nevertheless from the heart, deeply moving. Our services, organizations, special efforts, the sick—all are upheld by this little weekly gathering.

Other Evangelical contributions are the laying of great stress on home and overseas missions, and the seeking of better relationships with the Nonconformists, about which I have more to say later on. All these great positive things we Central Churchmen gratefully accept, but we utterly reject the unscholarly fundamentalism that demands that reason should be thrown overboard, the arbitrary rejection of certain inconvenient passages from the Book of Common Prayer, and the rather petty excitement about harmless amusements such as dancing and cards.

On the other hand, we have introduced a number of things that the Anglo-Catholics have stressed, just because they are absolutely right. Their greatest contribution has been the emphasis placed on the Holy Communion service as the central Sunday service, and in many a Central Churchmanship parish this has been or is being done without any sort of friction or difficulty. When things are absolutely right, with Biblical authority and the support of tradition, there is no real difficulty in introducing them provided that they are properly explained. I have introduced all sorts of so-called Anglo-Catholic practices here after very careful explanation and discussion, and I do not think we have lost one church member as a result.

The Anglo-Catholics have been responsible for the return of our Church to order and beauty and dignified ceremonial, and here I have introduced eastward position, candles on the altar, burses and veils and stoles at ordinary celebrations, and servers properly vested in albs and the wearing of the Eucharistic vestments in the four liturgical colours at the Family Communion. All these things were carefully explained, and we had quite a discussion about the introduction of vestments at a meeting of the Parochial Church Council, ending in an almost unanimous vote— and those who voted against explained to me that it was only because they felt the money should be spent on repairs and not on grounds of principle. This was how I put the whole matter in the magazine:

Why are we having vestments? The real reason is simply that our church badly needs the introduction of a little more colour and beauty. Every church ought to have beautiful things—pictures, woodwork, stained glass, silverware, brass, linen, materials, needlework, etc. At St. Ambrose's we have all too little. Art is used in the service of the church to offer to God the talents he has bestowed upon us. Our vestments will bring just this touch of beauty and colour and may be called ointment for the feet of Jesus. This is why we are having them and they have, in our view, no 'high church' significance whatsoever. It should be noted that their use is expressly authorized by the Ornaments Rubric printed just before the Order for Morning Prayer in your prayer book.

What are these vestments? Ambrosians are already used to the alb, amice and girdle worn by the servers. These will now be worn by the priest celebrating, with the addition o the chasuble, stole and maniple. Basically, vestments represent the long flowing garments worn in classical times by ordinary people in the Mediterranean countries. When, starting in the fourth century, they ceased to be worn and were replaced by more practical items of dress, the clergy continued to wear them at first both outside and inside and later only inside the churches.

The alb is the long white robe that used to be worn by all as the chief item of dress. It represents the long seamless robe worn by Jesus. The amice is the neckcloth. It represents the cloth used to blindfold Jesus. The girdle is worn around the waist and represents the ropes used to tie Jesus. The stole, worn over both shoulders by a priest and over the left one only by a deacon, is the napkin carried by servants and represents the yoke of Christ fully accepted by a priest and partly by a deacon. The maniple is worn over the left arm and represents the towel used by Jesus to dry the disciples' feet. The chasuble is the main part and is the outer garment (cape or cloak) that used to be worn. It represents the purple robe put on Jesus by the soldiers of Pilate.

From the Anglo-Catholics we accept a general reverence for history and tradition and a realization that ours is the historic Catholic Church of the realm, and we are grateful to them for all sorts of lesser things, such as the Christmas Crib and the Easter Garden, the observance of Candlemas, the blessing and distribution of palms on Palm Sunday, the observance of Saints Days and Holy Days, and the privilege of sacramental confession.

There is no difficulty about introducing any of these things provided that the incumbent is not touchy about the exercise of his prerogative and provided he does not regard it as somehow cowardly and unworthy to take his P.C.C. fully into his confidence. I told my P.C.C. at the outset that nothing of any importance would be done without their knowledge and general approval, and I have kept to this. The result has been general harmony and an absence of acrimonious criticism that might easily have resulted from high-handed action.

We Central Churchmen accept wholeheartedly these great contributions made by the Anglo-Catholics because they are so clearly true or supported by centuries of tradition or pastorally valuable, and because they add so much to the worthy offering of our worship to Almighty God. But we have no hesitation in rejecting the thoroughly bad things, the tiresome fussiness you sometimes see, the unlawful introduction of the interim rite, the plain disloyalty to the Book of Common Prayer, and the introduction of crude Latinisms such as the adoration of the Blessed Sacrament and non-communicating attendance at Holy Communion.

Old controversies are not dead, but they are surely dying. The Evangelicals came into being to stress certain things and they succeeded magnificently. They won their points, and now we all pay due regard to personal religion and we all attach the greatest importance to the Bible. The Anglo-Catholics endured mockery, humiliation, and worse for the sake of certain

B

vital principles—nearly all of which are now common-place and taken for granted. Almost every church has a weekly celebration of Holy Communion and reverent ceremonial, and order and dignity are found in churches of all points of view. There is really nothing very much left of any great importance for either side to get excited about. Both have won and neither has lost.

Perhaps it is still true that extreme Evangelicals want the Church of England to move towards what they consider to be the ideal reached long ago by the Methodists, and extreme Anglo-Catholics make that ideal Rome. Perhaps it is true that the former overdo the preaching of the Atonement, so that sermons repeat the theme of 'Brother, are you saved?' to the exclusion of much of value, while the Anglo-Catholic over-emphasis of the Incarnation leads to the curious practice of kneeling at the Incarnatus in the Creed and standing for the Cruci-fixion. Central Churchmanship sees the good and positive. We find much to admire in Nonconformity and in traditional Catholicism, and we preach both the Incarnation and the Atonement. In fact we keep the mean between the two extremes, and that this is, and has always been, the distinctive Anglican position is made clear by the opening words of the Preface to the Book of Common Prayer.

This positive Central Churchmanship, embodying the best of the Protestant and Catholic traditions, is what our working-class folk readily understand and want. In this position both strands come together, and this is seen most clearly in the widespread adoption of the Family Com-munion as the central Sunday service. I now want to describe ours, first of all describing what happens, and then how it was introduced and why.

CHAPTER THREE

THE CENTRE OF EVERYTHING

OUR Family Communion is the centre of everything here. Come along on a typical Sunday morning and see. The service begins at 9.55 a.m., but we have an earlier celebration at the usual 8 a.m., which is attended by a dozen or so: those who plan to go out for the day, or those who still like the quiet and stillness.

At 9 a.m. the bells start. A few like to come very early and these join the clergy in the side chapel to say Mattins at 9.30 a.m., a valuable preparation in itself, but having it at this time has another unanticipated consequence— it ensures reasonable quietness throughout the church and general reverence at a time of much activity. For much happens from 9.30 a.m. onwards. The church-wardens and some of the duty sidesmen are there, getting books out and ready to welcome the first arrivals. The organist and duty choirboys are there, getting everything ready in the choir. The servers have much to do. The women are busy in the kitchen getting the refreshments ready to serve in the big hall afterwards, and in that hall the children are putting out books and arranging things for their own service. A Mothers' Union member and two G.F.S. members or Guides are getting toys out for the nursery in the smaller hall, and those who give out the stamps for the day and mark the registers are in position.

By 9.50 a.m. people are coming thick and fast into church, and they include many young people and some complete families. Anything up to 200 adults and perhaps 150 children will be in church by the time the bells come down at 9.55 a.m., and then the banns are published and the organ plays until 10 a.m.

At 10 a.m. we sing the Mattins versicles and responses and the choir enters singing the *Venite*, or the *Benedicite* in Advent or Lent, or one of the other canticles or a psalm. They sing as they enter in procession, and this makes an ideal beginning. It also gets over one of the troubles about having a Family Communion—the people never otherwise hear the Mattins canticles. The celebrant (wearing vestments) and the two servers (wearing albs) say the preparatory prayers in the vestry and make a separate entrance.

Before the Communion service begins there may be some new members of one or other of the organizations to enrol, or perhaps a new choirboy to admit. These are great moments for them, and thus for the whole church family, and the ceremony takes only a few minutes. Although every minute counts and although great care has to be taken not to lengthen the service unduly, yet I feel sure this is the right time. Any dedications of new furnishings or new items also take place at this point.

We celebrate facing east, and we use the Sydney Nicholson setting, published by the Faith Press, never varying it from Sunday to Sunday. We chose this at the outset after considering Merbecke and Martin Shaw and several others, partly because good church musicians recommend it as musically beyond reproach and partly because it is so thoroughly congregational that all can and do join in. There is a further feature that I like very much—the descants for boys' voices. In this very lofty church the descants ringing out high above the rest sound simply magnificent. It is true that the organist and choir loudly clamour for a change from time to time, but so far we have resisted this pressure, and I think there is a lot to be said for a setting that everybody knows so well that they join in heartily.

The Collect for Purity is said by the whole congregation, the idea being to remind everybody that concentration and reverence is expected from all. It is not easy to get when you have a large number of young people present, not all of whom have been confirmed. There have been several sermons about this, and it has taken a long time to persuade the older members that the church is not a sort of club where you chat freely to your friends before, during, and after service. If young people see their elders talking they soon do it themselves, but this has now been more or less overcome and the general reverence is good, even amongst the children. The churchwardens fully intend to keep things that way, and are not above taking vigorous action at times if necessary.

The Ten Commandments are then sung, but we use a shorter version than is usual. The intention of the 1662 Prayer Book is that people shall hear the Ten Commandments in full every Sunday, and it seems to me to be a great pity that, in the interests of brevity, they have been cut out altogether in many churches. The variations permitted by the 1928 Prayer Book are useful and effective, but I do hold strongly that all our people need to have their attention drawn regularly to this ancient code of laws which, properly explained, is still entirely up to date. We shorten them as follows:

Celebrant:
> Thou shalt have none other Gods but me.
> Thou shalt not make to thyself any graven images . . . to worship them.
> Thou shalt not take the Name of the Lord thy God in vain.
> Remember the Sabbath Day to keep it holy.

Response:
> Lord have mercy upon us and incline our hearts to keep these laws.

Celebrant:
> Honour thy father and thy mother.
> Thou shalt do no murder.
> Thou shalt not commit adultery.
> Thou shalt not steal.

Thou shalt not bear false witness against thy neighbour.

Thou shalt not covet.

Response:

Lord have mercy upon us and write all these thy laws in our hearts we beseech thee.

Occasionally we use instead our Lord's Summary of the Law, but our people like to hear the Ten Commandments, and we have reason to know that our children and young people are becoming increasingly familiar with them.

The Epistle, usually read by the lay reader or a layman, is taken from Phillips's *Letters to Young Churches*, and some follow it in their Prayer Books and tell me afterwards that they understood some specially difficult passage for the first time. During the Gradual hymn the Gospel procession goes to the chancel step, and the people have been taught the meaning of this and see clearly the point of taking the Gospel out of the sanctuary into the world.

What happens after the Creed rather shakes our visiting preachers! While the organ plays there is a sort of general post. The children under secondary school age leave the church at this point, those under five going to the small hall where those looking after the babies are ready to receive them and keep them amused, and those over five going into the large hall which had been rigged as a church, and where their own service is held. Sometimes we use the film strip projector, sometimes a talk is given, always the stress is on worship. This service is usually taken by three laymen who take it very well, and they love doing this valuable piece of service. All children under secondary school age have to leave the church after the Creed unless they are with their parents, who must, of course, have the last word about the religious upbringing of their children. A few keep them throughout the service, but very few. I do not share the view of those who hold that children should stay throughout, bringing them to the altar with them to receive a blessing. It is simply not a service that is suitable for children. They may be interested where there is much movement, but the one thing we must not do is to bore them, and I find that the service of Holy Communion is, quite simply, beyond their understandings. Moreover, it is sound psychologically to give children something to which they can look forward. Our children are told that when they move up to secondary schools they are assumed to be capable of understanding deeper truths and they are told that this privilege is one to which they should eagerly look forward. Now and again we see rather young looking children staying throughout, and a reminder needs to be issued, but generally speaking the rule is accepted and the children much prefer their own service. Incidentally, the children are not the only ones who ought to be considered. If they get restless and disinterested the whole service is spoiled for their unfortunate mothers, and the devotions of others are interrupted too.

With the children gone, grown-ups from the side aisles move into the centre and the service continues. The sermon lasts ten minutes or so, and visiting preacher, who go on and on well beyond this limit are not popular because at this service the sermon is secondary.

The Offertory Procession is a great feature. Escorted by the churchwardens with their wands of office, the bread and wine and water, in addition to the money, are brought from the back of the church and the organist stops the hymn when the sidesmen reach the altar rail. All these things are offered with the words that the Scottish Prayer Book quotes from 1 Chronicles 29:

Thine, O Lord, is the greatness, and the power, and the glory, and the victory, and the majesty: for all that is in the heaven and in the earth is Thine; Thine is the kingdom, O Lord, and Thou art exalted as head above all. All things come of Thee and of Thine own have we given Thee.

These words are on a printed card stuck inside the back cover of each hymn book, and everybody joins in saying them.

Careful attention is given to the biddings before the Church Militant prayer, and we pray for the Church overseas, always remembering our own missionary by name, and the Church at home, before coming to local parish matters. Of course those in hospital and the chronic sick are remembered by name, and we commend into the hand of God members of the family who have passed on, using some more words printed on the card:

Priest: Rest eternal grant unto *him*, O Lord.
People: And let light perpetual shine upon *him*.

We found after the service that there were sometimes cases of sickness and even of death about which we knew nothing, so our procedure is now to put the list of intercessions at the back of the church so that worshippers can add names as they come in. This brings the list right up to date. Those who are prayed for by name in this way are often very deeply touched and very grateful, and they are encouraged, when they return, to give thanks by asking the celebrant to say something like 'Henry Smith desires to give thanks to Almighty God for a successful operation, and for restoration of health and strength.' The list is brought up with the offertory.

There is a sense of mounting expectancy as the service nears its climax, and the silence after the Consecration prayer is absolute.

Surely the 1662 Canon is absolutely right in not including the Prayer of Oblation and the Lord's Prayer immediately after it, thus making the silence possible at that supreme moment. The 1928 and the Scottish Canon seem to go on and on, and to me it spoils the whole thing.

For the administration we use two altars, and the churchwardens with their wands come out and control the traffic so that we never get large numbers standing in the aisles. Two priests and three laymen are required to administer. The Bishop of Bristol is always willing to license laymen of good standing to assist with the chalice when the application for such a licence is supported by a unanimous vote of the P.C.C. and where the need is genuine. We have to be realistic about this. With the five of us we can get through 175 communicants in eight minutes without unseemly haste, but when there is no assistant priest, when celebrant and two laymen have to do it all, it takes thirteen minutes, and that is too long when everybody is expected to remain kneeling unless feeling unwell. With one priest alone, with no lay assistance, the time becomes intolerably long and the whole service marred. Yet some bishops are rather hesitant about licensing laymen, and in New Zealand, for instance, this is never permitted under any circumstances. In some dioceses, London for one, special permission is given to lay readers, but an application has to be made every time such services are required.

We need to think hard about this. In many parishes Family Communion is now the central service of the day, but it is often remarked that there seems to be a sort of 'sound barrier' at about the 200 mark, and the fact is that in few parishes do you find 300 or 400 communicants every Sunday at one service. What is the reason for this? I believe the time taken for the administration has a great deal to do with it. People are kneeling from the beginning of the *Benedictus* and through the Prayers of Humble Access and Consecration right up to the time when they come forward to the altar rail. Here we all stand for the *Sursum Corda* and until the *Sanctus*, and this makes a welcome break. But in spite of this the communicants at the back of the church may well have to remain kneeling for twenty minutes before they come to the altar rail. Where the numbers are far greater than ours this time is obviously greatly exceeded, and our ordinary church people just do not have the spiritual resources to occupy such a long period of time with their

B*

own private devotions. This very long period can, and does, spoil the service.

Can anything be done about it? One answer would be communion in one kind, and this is the established Roman Catholic practice and enables the Roman Catholic celebrant to communicate hundreds of people in a very short space of time. It is, however, open to the grave objections that it is opposed to Scripture and tradition, and is thus thoroughly un-Anglican. Very few of us would approve of the introduction of such a practice, remembering that one of the achievements of the Reformation was to restore communion in both kinds.

Another and better way would be to allow laymen to administer the paten as well as the chalice. The actual administration of the elements is surely in no sense a distinctively priestly function, and if lay readers can be permitted by Convocation to administer the chalice there is no obvious reason why they should not be permitted to perform both functions. If this privilege can be given to lay readers, then it could surely be given also to laymen who are not lay readers but who are of good standing in the parish.

Justin Martyr tells us that in the second century the deacons used to take the Eucharistic elements to those prevented from attending the Eucharist in person, and whatever the precise functions of deacons in the second century may have been, they were certainly not priestly as we understand that term. There is thus unquestionable historical precedent for the practice, and there are very sound practical reasons why it should be adopted now. The objections to it are surely based on pure prejudice, and the view may well be that our lay folk would not welcome such an introduction. If that is so it may be of interest to state that our laymen here who are licensed to administer the chalice consider it to be a very great privilege to be allowed to do so, and they do it with the greatest possible reverence and dignity. In the six years that I have been here I have not had one single objection to their doing so from any member of my congregation, young or old.

One consequence of the present shortage of priests is that we are rediscovering the theology of the laity as the people of God, and the dividing line between priestly and lay functions is becoming steadily less defined. I suggest it is high time that we encouraged laymen of good standing to help in this way, and to do something that would be of the greatest practical help in building up the Family Communion into the great service of the day.

Everybody joins in saying the prayer of Thanksgiving, and the service ends soon after 11 a.m. The children's service ends at the same time, and we move into the church hall for tea and biscuits, served by the duty team of caterers. Adults pay 3d. for a cup of tea and biscuit, and children 2d., and this shows a small profit that is useful for paying for refreshments on those occasions when no charge is made (Chapter meetings, for instance). Parents and children come together, and in this cheerful social atmosphere we meet as friends. Newcomers can soon be made to feel at home and can be introduced to others. The notices are given out in a more informal way than is possible in church, tickets are sold, club secretaries can make any special announcements. We find the time afterwards to be ideal for meetings involving mostly men, and our football and cricket clubs and Church of England Men's Society meet on Sundays at 11.30 a.m., and so do some of our committees. The women like to get home and get on with the dinner preparations.

Newcomers, I said, can be made to feel at home—but 'can' is the operative word. The natural and immediate tendency is to form little groups and the regular members tend to ignore them. I often see newcomers standing alone. Our people do not shine at the social graces, and there is a certain diffidence and shyness about approaching strangers and making light conversation, the sort of thing that is supposed to be one of our national

characteristics and is commonly found in railway compart-
ments. It is here. But it is breaking down. Newcomers
who are not put off, but who continue to come, soon find
themselves treated as members of the family.

Here, then, is the centre of everything, from which
everything comes and to which everything leads. It is
the Central Churchmanship combination of the Protestant
Breaking of Bread and the Catholic High Mass, and it
includes the most valuable features of both. Our people
deeply love it and understand it. We stick closely to the Book
of Common Prayer, adding the *Benedictus* and the *Agnus Dei*.
These permitted additions are printed in the little booklet
The Service of Holy Communion, published by the S.P.C.K.,
price 6*d*., which we give to everybody present to enable
them to follow everything easily. The whole congregation
joining in in saying certain parts of the service normally
said by the celebrant alone makes the service more
congregational and this is specially important when a
good choir is there to lead the singing. It has to be made
abundantly clear that the choir is singing not to the
congregation but to God, and there is one thing that we
have recently introduced that makes this very clear.
We have an anthem sung by the choir during the actual
administration. It is always very carefully prepared and
faultlessly sung, and it does add something to the service.
The sheer beauty of it adds to the solemnity of this particular moment. But we leave nothing else to the choir
alone. Everybody is urged to make their contribution
both in the sung and in the spoken parts of the service.

All this began in a very quiet sort of way on my
very first Sunday, with seventy-one communicants. It
remained like that, with an average of about sixty-five
communicants, until the first Confirmation nine months
later when the average went up to something over the
hundred. It has gone up steadily, and now we average
something like 175 communicants; a good many more
than this for a few months after the annual Confirmation
and a good many less during the summer months. There

is usually a number of interested inquirers not yet confirmed, and it is always an inspiration to look from the altar at a well-filled church.

Now we must consider the why and the how.

CHAPTER FOUR

WHY THE FAMILY COMMUNION?

THE pattern in many a working-class parish still tends to be a very small morning congregation and a larger evening one. I felt absolutely certain that this had to be changed when I came here because evening worship is likely to decrease as the years go by. Living standards are going up. Cars are becoming more and more numerous, and I can take you to modest streets here where a dozen or more cars are parked every night by their council house owners. People who have cars want to use them, and trips to the countryside and the coast are becoming the usual Sunday practice of increasing numbers. This is already beginning to affect not only Sunday evening worship, but Sunday afternoons as well, and large afternoon Sunday schools seem to be on the way out. Even the Methodists, supreme masters of the Sunday school technique, report a marked fall in the numbers of children attending and increasing difficulty in finding teachers. There are additional factors. Sunday cinemas take away numbers of people who might otherwise attend a Sunday evening service, and now television provides a strong inducement to stay at home on Sunday evenings.

The religious broadcasts usually take place on television at the normal time of evening service, and millions watch them. We do not mind in the least, indeed we welcome such a potent ally, because the main appeal is to the fringer. But it stands out a mile that it simply will not do to be content with small morning congregations, a good afternoon Sunday school, and a well-attended evening service. In the summer you have the rival claims of the beaches and the open air, and in the winter you have the cinemas and television, and I feel strongly that it is vital that the chief stress should be laid on Sunday morning worship for adults and children alike, simply on grounds of expediency.

And I wanted to see family worship, using 'family' in a double sense. Families that pray together stay together, and with so much in our way of life to divide and break up the family it is surely vital that religion should bind together. I wanted to see fathers and mothers and children coming together, and I was determined to do everything I possibly could to make this possible. Every congregation is a family, and I wanted to make members here conscious of the fact.

The only question that remained to be decided was which morning service should it be, Holy Communion or Mattins? I was brought up on Mattins. I love this service, and always will. But Churchmen of all degrees are coming to see more and more clearly that the New Testament and history alike put the Lord's Own Service on the Lord's Own Day in the first place.

When Jesus said: 'Do this in remembrance of me' He implied continuing action, and was so understood by the Apostles themselves. Acts 2[42] shows that from the beginning this breaking of bread was regularly observed in obedience to this command, and it is fascinating to see from early documents how the service developed from the simple and extempore to the fixed canon. The *Didache* (c. A.D. 100) gives instructions about the words to be used when celebrating, and places the main emphasis on thanksgiving all the way through, adding that only the baptized may receive Communion and ordering the unrepentant to be excluded. Incidentally, would it not be possible to include in any future revision that lovely prayer from this work:

Glory be to Thee for ever. As this bread that is broken was scattered upon the mountains, and gathered together, and become one, so let Thy Church be gathered together from the ends of the earth into Thy kingdom: for Thine is the glory and the power through Jesus Christ for ever.

Justin in his *Apology* (*c*. A.D. 163) gives much more detailed information and tells us that the service is called Eucharist and held every Sunday, because on that day Jesus rose from the dead. He outlines the doctrine of the Real Presence and stresses the Amen after the Prayer of Consecration that is said to indicate assent by all present. He says that the service begins with readings from the records of the Apostles or the writings of the Prophets, and this is followed by some instruction and exhortation by the president. The offertory is for the poor and needy.

It is clear that from the earliest days the service of Holy Communion was central in East and West alike, and it is still, of course, the great central service of the Roman Catholic and Eastern Orthodox Churches on the one hand and of the Plymouth Brethren and the Gospel Halls on the other. Calvin took the same view, for he wrote: 'The Lord's Supper should be celebrated in the Christian congregation once a week at the very least.'

There is no evidence that at the Reformation the English reformers ever meant to depart from this unanimous verdict of history. It is true that they wanted to abolish the Romish sacrifice of the Mass. But they simply wanted to put in its place something much better—a scriptural Communion service, corporate and congregational, with the preaching of the Word integral.

The Prayer Book itself makes this clear, for it is in Holy Communion alone that provision is made for the giving out of church notices, the preaching of a sermon, and the taking of the collection. The intention was that Morning Prayer and Litany should come first as a preparation, but that everybody should regard the Holy Communion as a regular weekly obligation with a communicating attendance.

It was by an accident of history that Mattins came to be the chief service. For centuries English people had heard Mass, only making their Communions very infrequently—once a year on Easter Day was considered adequate. And they simply refused to change quite suddenly to making it every Sunday. They walked out instead of staying, and our Church bowed to the seemingly inevitable, dressed up Mattins by the addition of a penitential beginning and the state prayers at the end, added a sermon and the notices and hymns, and gradually dropped regular celebrations of Holy Communion, until three times a year became the maximum rather than the minimum. In the eighteenth century there were some churches that never had any celebrations, and in our Church generally the Holy Communion was pushed right out into the background. It was not until the nineteenth-century Oxford Movement that it became a regular Sunday service again.

In most parish churches there is a regular weekly celebration but it is still far from being the chief service in many of them. Puzzled confirmation candidates are told during their instruction that this really is the most important service of all—and when they come at 8 a.m. they find only a tiny number of worshippers. Perhaps the crowning indignity is when the service follows Mattins and three-quarters of the worshippers make for the door, suggesting that it is a sort of voluntary extra for the specially pious. There is something wrong with both the early and the late celebrations when they are attended only by a minority, and when they ignore the deliberate stress laid by the reformers upon the unity of the ministry of the Word and the sacraments.

One of the most encouraging things in this twentieth century is the general return by all schools of thought from Evangelical to Anglo-Catholic to the Parish Communion, and it was clear to me that I had to introduce this service at once as the chief service of the day. I never had any doubts about this being entirely right in the light of Scripture and tradition and the intention of the reformers, and as the years go by the service comes to mean more and more to me. My people tell me that it means more and more to them as well. This is to be expected because this service has everything. The two aspects treasured by the Protestants and Non-conformists are memorial and fellowship, and these are vividly presented by our liturgy. We make our solemn act of remembrance of the events of the Last Supper and all that followed as we have been commanded to do. It is hard to visualize any more effective demonstration of the real fellowship that unites us than the sharing of a common plate and a common cup at a common meal. The two aspects treasured by Catholics are sacrifice and thanksgiving, and these are present in full measure. We offer ourselves, all that we are and all that we have. The note of thanksgiving runs through the whole service, coming to a climax at the end.

This service has everything. Protestant and Catholic alike should find something familiar, and I share the view that this service is doing more than anything else to bring about not only that unity that is desperately needed in our own Church, but also the final unity of all the Churches. There is something else that it has that I had not previously suspected. It is a converting agency. The Wesleys long ago regarded it as such, and I have found it to be true. When you make this your central service all sorts of people come along from varied motives, possibly just to hear the banns read or to see young Albert enrolled as a choirboy. There are sometimes surprising results and I have a number of most faithful communicants whose starting point was here. Jesus Christ crucified is set before their eyes and they are brought face to face with the fact of the Gospel. Some of them have this experience for the first time, and it leads them to desire to find out more and go farther.

The very keystone of the strategy that I am recommending is the introduction of the Parish Communion. It probably means the sacrificing of certain things. It means pushing Mattins into the background, a real

wrench for those who love this service. It means abandon-
ing the principle of fasting Communion, a discipline
that many of us have learned to value. It means the loss
of those quiet minutes on Sundays at 8 a.m. for those
who have treasured them for years. I do not think any
compromise is really effective. Some, I know, have their
Parish Communion at a comparatively early hour such
as 9 a.m., so that fasting is still possible, but such a service
can never become the focal point of the whole parish,
and there are all sorts of snags. 10 a.m. is probably
about right in most parishes. You simply cannot get
the Sunday school children there much earlier than that
because most of them come from semi-pagan homes
where the parents resent being disturbed at what they
consider to be a very early hour. You must not be any
later, because mother has to get the dinner ready. The
service is far too long for fasting attendance, and if
fasting is encouraged many will either fail to concentrate
or will pass clean out. If you abandon fasting attendance
you lose something but not anything absolutely vital.
The practice has surely been stressed to ensure proper
preparation. Our Church has never insisted on it, and
there are other ways of preparing, such as informing the
incumbent the day before, as the first rubric insists. We
can teach our confirmation candidates about the need
for preparation, and we need not assume that non-
fasting attendance indicates unprepared reception. Set
against this loss all the gains. Whole families can attend,
babies included, because mother has time to get the
children ready. Children and young people of all ages
are there who would not be there if the service was an
hour earlier. Reverence and concentration on the deepest
mysteries of all are possible. The service can and does
become the centre of the whole parish. The losses are
small when compared with the gains.

These, then, are the reasons why I introduced the
Parish Communion, or rather the Family Communion.
I prefer the term 'Family' because it seems to me to have

a deeper meaning and one that is clearly and easily understood. It is, however, one thing to have the idea clear in one's mind, but quite another to get the whole thing across, particularly in a parish that has had only Conservative Evangelical traditions. The task proved to be easier than I had expected.

CHAPTER FIVE

THE TEACHING

MORE than twenty years ago I was priest-in-charge of a new housing area in Devonport, with a small wooden church serving the needs of 10,000 people. After reading and being deeply impressed by a little book called *Sunday Morning: The New Way*, by Brother Edward, I wanted to introduce the Family Communion. The trouble was that hardly any lay folk had ever heard of this sort of service, and it was somehow thought that 11 a.m. was the only possible time for the chief morning service. I had great difficulty in persuading my rector that it was a good thing and an experiment well worth trying, and the deciding factor was that everybody came in the evening and hardly anybody to Mattins. At any rate, he considered, I could not do much harm, and agreed to my trying it out at 9.30 a.m., provided that Mattins followed at 11 a.m. as usual.

What a performance it was! For six months I preached and taught and visited and stressed Family Communion *ad nauseam*. Finally we fixed the date of the first service. A personal visit had to be paid to every choir member, and a rather reluctant promise obtained to make the 9.30 a.m. service the first obligation, at any rate for a few weeks. I got the names of fifty people who promised faithfully to come to the first one. All the uniformed organizations were asked to parade on the great day, to give some further support by their presence. Everybody thought the new plan was some queer idea of the priest-in-charge, and one that was bound to fail. It did not fail. The first service was a wonderful experience with over one hundred communicants, and we never looked back.

But that was twenty-two years ago. Nowadays everybody has at least heard of the Family Communion, and it is pretty certain that most of them have been to one. The idea is not regarded as novel or high church or low church. Accordingly there seemed to me to be no point in delaying matters, and I announced that the change over would take place on my first Sunday, the choir being asked to learn the Nicholson music thoroughly before my arrival. My predecessor had taught his confirmation candidates the importance of Holy Communion, and he had had a regular choral Communion on one Sunday each month instead of Mattins, just like many other faithful Evangelical incumbents. The Parochial Church Council had agreed to the change that they knew I proposed making, and I asked them to make a point of coming *en bloc* to the first service. They did so and the quiet beginning was thought to be encouraging, but take away the choir members and the P.C.C. and the few who used to come to Mattins (and who readily made the change) there were not many others present and the vast church looked pretty empty. We had the framework at the outset, built by others. My real job had begun.

This small but faithful nucleus had been taught by my predecessor the great Evangelical aspects of memorial and fellowship. The P.C.C. was solidly behind me. If there were some who objected to the new way, and who resented the displacement of Mattins and the substitution of the Family Communion, then they kept quiet about it and nothing in the way of controversy divided us, although I learned later on that some were not very happy about this implication of Central Churchmanship. They came, however, out of loyalty to their church, and for no other reason. And as they began to appreciate the deeper meaning of this service, and as they saw new people coming into our fellowship, they changed their views and became enthusiastic supporters.

It was teaching that was required. I had to turn the faithful few into instructed, outward-looking missionaries who were conscious of being members of a family or worshipping fellowship and who were able and willing to tell others.

I have before me the sermons that I preached at an early stage at the Family Communion, and a summary of them may be of interest.

1. THE BACKGROUND. Why is this service more important than any other? Why is this the chief service in the Roman Catholic Church and in the Eastern Orthodox Church and in many a humble Gospel Hall? It is because this service was ordered by Jesus Himself when He said: 'Do this in remembrance of Me.' It simply will not do to make this service a little quiet affair attended by a little handful in the early mornings. It has always been in intention THE service of the day—and this is what we are going to make it here.

We call it our Family Communion partly because we want it to be our weekly family gathering, with every member of our church present, and partly because we want to see whole families, mother, father and children, coming every Sunday.

Make sure you know all your fellow-members of the St. Ambrose family. Look around you and see who is present and who absent, and do not hesitate to go and call on the absent ones and find out what is wrong and show them that they have been missed. And be sure to come to the social gathering afterwards and hear the notices and discuss church affairs, and over tea and biscuits meet old friends and make new ones. Do please see that strangers are welcomed and that nobody feels out of things.

This is our great weekly meeting. Gradually our customs will become more and more familiar, and out of loyalty to your church please accept them when you understand them, and let us have everybody doing the same thing in the same way. This service is going to be the centre of everything here, and it will soon be just that if you see how vital it is that you and your whole family should be present every Sunday unless prevented from coming by something really unavoidable. If you 'belong' that should be your rule and nothing less will do.

2. THE PREPARATION. St. Paul says it is possible to eat and to drink to our own damnation. Preparation has always been insisted on, for this is something that must be taken seriously, with careful examination the night before, being ruthless as we see ourselves as we really are, sinners in need of grace. Read through the Collect, Epistle and Gospel. Come early and think quietly, never talking to anybody in church. Then see how the service itself helps us to prepare for the great climax.

The Collect for Purity and the cry for mercy that follows it represent the preparation of our hearts and wills, that we want cleansed before we go any farther. The Epistle, Gospel, Creed and Address are meant to prepare our minds, because there is something to learn at every service, and here there is a special point every Sunday. The Confession and Absolution prepare the conscience and with that clear, with the slate wiped clean, we proceed to the very heart of the service. It is impossible to be worthy partakers, but we are bound to try to make ourselves as worthy as we possibly can, and we do this by careful preparation.

3. OUR OFFERING. See in the Old Testament the idea of offering sacrifices to God. This deeply rooted instinct finds its expression here, for true worship is giving rather than getting. What do we offer? We offer bread and wine, symbols of the necessities of life, symbols of the labours of men's hands, involving, when you come to think of it, ships and sailors, farms and farm workers, transport, machines, tool-makers, clerks in offices and hosts of others. We offer the labour of our hands. We also offer our money, although it used to be in kind.

We offer something else—ourselves, our souls and bodies. This means pledging ourselves to His service, for He bought us with His blood and we belong to Him and on our brows we bear His sign that was placed there at Baptism. Those who understand that this whole service is one great offering of all that we have, and are, and hope to be, will soon see it to be a weekly necessity taking precedence over all else.

4. THE CONSECRATION. We offer our unworthy gifts. God accepts them and transforms them and gives back to us something infinitely precious. The elements of bread and wine become possessed of a new meaning and value in fact during

the Prayer of Consecration, the great climax of the service, in accordance with the words of Jesus at the Institution. How does it happen? This is a mystery, but it may be helpful to look at this small piece of paper that we call a pound note. By virtue of the signature of the chief cashier of the Bank of England this small piece of paper is declared to have a value that it did not possess before, the value of twenty shillings. It really has. And so with the elements in Holy Communion. They are declared to have the value of the body and blood of Christ, by the authority of the properly ordained priest celebrating, and we believe that Jesus is specially present wherever the Holy Communion is being celebrated. The sun's rays can be focused by a million magnifying glasses thousands of miles apart and those rays thus concentrated in many places. So Jesus can be present wherever this is happening.

Here earth and heaven are linked. The thought of the Western Church is that heaven is brought to earth and the thought of the Eastern Church is that earth is lifted up to heaven. On the one hand, Christ comes to us and takes and breaks and blesses our offerings, using the priest as His mouthpiece. On the other hand we are caught up into heaven to share with angels and archangels in the worship that is being continually offered. The two thoughts are blended in our liturgy and East and West come together. 'Lift up your hearts' says the priest, and we lift them up, right up into heaven. Of course we stand. We join in the song of the angels with our 'Holy, Holy, Holy.' And then we remember how earth-bound we are as we kneel for the *Benedictus*; and the Prayer of Humble Access is a reminder that we are not worthy to offer anything.

It is through His mercy and not of our deserving that we are permitted, nevertheless, to come to the Upper Room. As the priest breaks the bread, please remember the body that was once broken for us and remember that our bodies too may have to be broken for Him. Remember that something tremendous happens at that moment and join clearly and firmly in the Amen that makes that Prayer of Consecration your own. Then in the silence give thanks that the Lamb of God has truly come.

5. THE COMMUNION. We have been going through the service of Holy Communion to see the wonderful meaning of it. I want you to be filled with awe and wonder. When you are, it will not be necessary to ask anybody to stop whispering or gazing around because you will be thinking of the deepest mysteries of our religion and feel the movement as we offer our gifts, as God accepts them and as He gives them back to us.

After the Prayer of Consecration there is a deep silence, followed by the singing of the *Agnus Dei*. Then you come forward. As you come you should say, 'Lord, I am not worthy,' and you can repeat this as you receive. As you return remember that these things are not meant for the faithful few, for the specially pious, but for all, and ask yourself what you can do to make this known.

The Sea of Galilee is pure and crystal clear because it receives the waters of Jordan and passes them on. The Dead Sea lives up to its name because it receives but does not pass on. What can you do? Some can organize and help run the many organizations that we long to start. Some can speak a word in season. Some can bear silent witness. All can help and all must be conscious of the duty to lead others to Christ. That broken bread symbolizes giving all the way.

The service ends with the Lord's Prayer and the Prayer of Oblation or Thanksgiving and the *Gloria in Excelsis*, which together make up a harmony of triumphant praise. We leave after the Blessing with our hearts filled with the deepest thanksgiving. Out we go with our family sense renewed, our faith re-kindled, our sins forgiven, our whole selves cleansed and refreshed, our enthusiasm and sense of mission deeply stirred. We have given, God has accepted, He has given back to us. Out we go, to be His Church, His body on earth, the body through which alone He can speak and act and reach others.

As summer drew near I took the opportunity of saying something about the customs that had already become firmly established here by an article in the magazine about going to church on holiday:

Do not worry about the differences you find in movement and ceremonial. In some churches the drill is far more

complicated and elaborate than anything you are used to
here. In some again an austere simplicity will be found.
In all you will find the same Book of Common Prayer, the
same Holy Communion service, the same Lord present in the
elements of bread and wine. You will make your Communion
with your fellow disciples in just the same way everywhere.

There are some things that we do here that you do not
find everywhere, and a word or two about them may be
helpful.

1. THE GOSPEL PROCESSION. Several of you have told me
that you like this custom that we have recently introduced.
The servers take the Gospel book out of the sanctuary, out of
the chancel to the chancel step, and the Gospel is read from
there. There is, of course, a definite purpose here, a deep
significance presented in dramatic form. We receive so much
in church, we receive supremely at the altar rail. Then what?
The Gospel procession is meant to be a reminder that it simply
will not do just to think about receiving. What we receive in
church we must take out with us into the world.

2. THE OFFERTORY PROCESSION. There is a great dignity
about this impressive procession every Sunday. The churchwardens lead the way. Then sidesmen carry the wine,
water and bread from the back of the church. Other sidesmen
bring the collection. The name of this procession makes the
meaning clear—we are offering something back to God. We
offer back to Him the things He so freely bestows upon us.
We offer our money, symbolic of the wages we earn. A part
is given every week by all of us for the work of God. We offer
to Him the bread and wine that will be transformed by Him
and given back to us changed with a new meaning. The bread
and wine have been made by many people. The farmer has
played his part, so has the engineer who made the combine
harvester and the tractor that pulls it, or perhaps the sailor
who helped to bring the wheat from overseas. We offer to
God all our talents, all our skill, and all our industry. It is a
sort of Harvest Festival every Sunday morning.

3. THE 'DO' AFTERWARDS. Nearly everybody comes into
the hall for tea and biscuits afterwards, and to hear the
notices, and a very pleasant little gathering we have for
twenty minutes or so. Old worshippers can meet and welcome

newcomers. Friends can meet and greet each other. Bonds of fellowship are strengthened and our church made that much more effective. Nobody can ever say: 'I used to go to St. Ambrose, but nobody ever spoke to me'—at least, if they do it is their own fault! By the way, those of you who do not like a social gathering of this sort, but prefer to go straight home, should remember that we are trying to break down something, this awful indifference to other worshippers that for years has been a grievous weakness of our church. This is meant to be a family gathering—and such a gathering is not complete if some of the members are missing.

These are some of the features that you may or may not find at a Family Communion in another church on holiday. And there are others. You may not find a service for children running at the same time. You may not find a nursery for very young children. You may not find a willing army of volunteers doing the work involved in serving refreshments. Here at St. Ambrose we owe a special debt of gratitude to those who miss the service by helping with the nursery and children's service.

One final word while I am on this subject. Of course, adults who are not confirmed can attend this service. Lots do. We often see couples there who want to hear their banns read, curious ones who wonder what the service is all about, Roman Catholics who are thinking of joining up with us, and adults who are seriously considering Confirmation. Let them all come. This is our Lord's own service. He is the host. He it is who welcomes us all.

This is the sort of teaching that helped to build up the Family Communion and to make it into the central Sunday service. It all began quietly, but although the average was only sixty-five communicants a Sunday for the first nine months, until the first Confirmation, yet the attendance steadily began to mount. Good numbers of children began to come, and some brought their parents with them. Those who began coming to confirmation classes were asked to make a point of being present every Sunday. The strategy outlined farther on began to produce results.

Here I should make it plain that it has not been roses all the way. Although there is so much to encourage we also have had, and still have, our heartbreaks and set backs, and the following figures will show the sort of thing I mean:

Year	Confirmation candidates		Still faithful	
	Under 18	Over 18	Under 18	Over 18
1954 ..	nil			
1955 ..	32	32	18	18
1956 ..	32	15	20	10
1957 ..	27	28	18	16
1958 ..	24	18	20	7
1959 ..	27	10	27	8
1960 ..	48	8	48	8

Year	Easter Day communicants	Total communicants
1953 ..	178	2,377
1954 ..	201	4,106
1955 ..	273	7,696
1956 ..	300	8,676
1957 ..	321	9,521
1958 ..	322	10,652
1959 ..	321	10,221
1960 ..	339	

It will be noticed that of 301 candidates presented for Confirmation, eighty-three are no longer active. Forty have left the parish, and some of them are regular worshippers at other churches, but the others have just dropped away. It is difficult to say why, but the chief cause is leaving school and facing criticisms and not always very friendly banter at work, and some teenagers just throw their hands in. The introduction of a Family Communion does not solve this most heartbreaking problem, although it does help, as witness the fact that the boys and girls confirmed several years ago are still mostly faithful. But some still drop away. Nor does this service ensure regular attendance every Sunday in spite of all the teaching given and the stress laid on this duty. There are perhaps 120 or so who do in fact rarely miss, but others are more erratic and require careful shepherding.

It will be noticed that the figures for 1959 show that the steady increase has ceased; indeed, we were back by 431 communicants. There are several reasons for this; for instance, the fact that in 1959 All Saints' Day and our Dedication Festival (November 15th) both fell on a Sunday, and we thus did not have our usual weekday evening Choral Communions on these days. But the conclusion is really that we seem to be right in the 'sound barrier' already mentioned that seems to operate in parishes that make the Family Communion their central service of the day. We are certainly not going to accept about 175 communicants a Sunday as our maximum average figure, and I feel convinced, with so many promising young people coming along, that we are bound to break through and get much greater numbers than this in due course. But the problem of lengthy administration is undoubtedly a factor making the task more difficult.

The Family Communion is no easy answer to every problem; indeed, it raises several new ones. It makes coming to Holy Communion a very easy matter, and the old discipline of getting up early, itself very valuable, no longer obtains. Moreover, it would be naïve to suppose that all who do come do so after careful preparation. Some prepare in the way suggested, and some do not. Quite a few who come have not got a clue about the meaning of this most solemn of all services, and this is a consequence of making it the chief service of the day.

These are real worries and matters for deep concern. The answer I think is that very many do prepare seriously and grow in grace. It is not quite so easy as is sometimes supposed, even if early rising is not involved, when you consider the homes from which some of the youngsters come and the kind of thing they have to put up with at work. We have to ask ourselves also whether the Holy Communion service is only intended for the pious few. If we believe that it is meant for sinners in need of grace, that nobody is worthy, then it follows that all must be welcome, and it would be quite wrong to discourage the uninstructed. Here we are delighted when Teddy boys and all sorts of unlikely characters come along, and the fact is that this service can speak to them in a truly wonderful way.

The only easy thing about the Family Communion is introducing it. The hard work then begins, hard work coupled with love and patience and the best use of limited time. A clear and definite strategy is needed to build up from small beginnings, and this we must now look at in closer detail.

PART TWO

THE STRATEGY IN DETAIL

CHAPTER SIX

THE ORGANIZATIONS

THE first thing is to get the Family Communion started. I am quite clear that this must always be the right thing to do in any working-class parish, for the reasons already given, and I feel pretty confident that it may also be right in a good many other types of parish as well, but that is outside the scope of this book. It is easy enough simply to announce that this will in future be the chief service, and it is certain that there will be an encouraging response, whether the previous traditions have been 'high' or 'low,' provided that the P.C.C. (and this I believe to be vital) has undertaken to support it. It is easy to get together Sunday by Sunday the faithful few. The real problem is to reach out to the others.

This is where we have to have a clear strategy and stick to it at all costs, being prepared to face unpopularity and misrepresentation, for this is the price that will surely have to be paid. We have to reach out to others, to be missionary leaders, because you cannot make bricks without straw, and you cannot make converts unless you use every opportunity presented. Put in another way and using a phrase that has the highest authority, we have to land our fish. Why are we so diffident about this? I decided at the outset that my job was to get my people to be outward looking and to get them to help me to extend the kingdom of God right here. The offering to God of the worship due to Him must be as worthy as we can possible make it, but there is surely something wrong when this offering is made only by a tiny minority. I had to lead people to a personal acceptance of Jesus Christ as Lord and Saviour, and then frankly to face the consequences of that acceptance. I wanted to see confirmation candidates of all ages coming forward for preparation and then taking their places in the fellowship and becoming regular communicants and growing in grace, and in turn leading others in. There must be nothing vague and general here. Everybody knows the story of the angler on the river bank who was asked by a passer-by whether he had caught any fish. 'No,' he replied, 'but I think I have influenced several!' In that setting the whole attitude is patently ridiculous, but is it any less so in a religious setting? I believe we are too vague altogether about this in our general reluctance to talk religion, and in our dread of putting people off. I heard it said at a meeting the other day that our guidance should be 'non-directional' when we meet people for marriage interviews or baptism arrangements. I believe this to be a wholly wrong approach.

The next thing was to tidy up the existing church organizations, and this meant making myself the most disliked man in the neighbourhood amongst the non-churchgoers, because some pretty drastic action was called for. The St. Ambrose Men's Club was first on the list. This club occupied the smaller church hall permanently, having three full-sized billiards tables there, and thus making it useless for any other purpose. The annual meeting was delayed until my arrival, and I found at this meeting that only three members had anything to do with the church. I told the members that the club must close forthwith, and I gave them three months to dispose of the tables, pointing out that the halls were meant for church purposes and the money to build them had been given with this in mind. They were not meant to provide the cheapest billiards in East Bristol, nor for the recreation of all and sundry. This decision was not well received by the members, and the local tradesmen who were members promptly withdrew their advertisements from the parish magazine just to indicate disapproval!

The Badminton Club had also waited for my arrival.
This club occupied the large hall on one evening a week,
and again I inquired at the annual meeting how many
members were connected with the church. The answer
was again three. This club was, I was told, one of the
best in Bristol, with teams in the first and second divisions
of the league, and I was told how proud I should be to
see the name of the church appear in the local paper
with such credit. This failed to impress me, and I told
this club to look for other premises as quickly as possible
because, although I wanted to have a Badminton Club,
I wanted one confined to church members.

The Scouts and Guides came in for close scrutiny.
They were orderly and well run, and meeting a real
need but, being 'open' companies, they were not confined
to St. Ambrose children, and it soon became clear that
the members of our own Sunday school were in a
minority. Other children were attached to every church
in the vicinity or to no church at all, and the only rule
was monthly attendance at church parade. I gave
instructions that in future only members of our own
church were to be admitted, thus ensuring that with the
passing of time the companies would become genuine
St. Ambrose ones. And this went for the Cubs and
Brownies too.

I was not very happy about the Bible Classes meeting
on Sunday afternoons. There were two, one for women
of all ages and one for youths. The worrying thing about
them was that both were clearly church substitutes, for
the members told me frankly that they did not come to
ordinary church services, and reckoned that coming in
the afternoons was enough for anybody. Both were
speedily closed down.

I began to feel like the young Westcott House man
who came to Canon B. K. Cunningham with this interesting account of his ministry: 'I have emptied two churches,
Professor, and now by God's grace I hope to empty a
third!' I did not at all enjoy all this 'getting tough' with

the very people I most wanted to get alongside, and it was not made any easier by having to do the job entirely alone. It would, I feel sure, have been wrong to have brought the P.C.C. into it and thus escaped the final responsibility. The prerogative was mine alone. Naturally the whole matter was talked out at length afterwards, and the interesting thing was that the P.C.C. entirely supported me. Many of the members had felt strongly that it was wrong that a men's club should occupy a church hall at a purely nominal rent of £40 a year, a figure which covered all lighting and heating. They were not at all happy about a Badminton Club that was St. Ambrose only in name, and there was general approval amongst church members. The anger was mostly confined to the displaced club members, and was not really shared very strongly by parishioners generally.

I had to tread very warily with the leaders of the Scouts and Guides and Bible Classes, and I did nothing until I had explained very carefully just what I meant to do, and why, pointing out that I had something constructive in mind. I explained that it was quite wrong to seek to bring in new church members via organizations, partly because it seemed to me less than honest, and partly because the method quite clearly had not worked in the past, nor was likely to work in the future. I explained that the organizations were meant to cater for the needs of the church members of all ages, and I wanted them to be an extension of the Family Communion. Those who worshipped together should join together for instruction, fellowship, and recreation in buildings built and maintained by church members. These leaders, splendid people all of them, accepted this and loyally undertook to carry out the new rules. It may be of interest that the Scouts were down to eight members when I arrived but, far from decreasing, the membership is now thirty, all church members. None of the other organizations has suffered in numbers, but there is a general gain in quality. This system of 'closed' organizations, i.e. organizations open only to existing church members, has another advantage of great importance in a town parish. It avoids difficulties with neighbouring churches. The ministers of the local chapels around here used to get very put out when their Sunday school children were obliged to attend our monthly church parades, and thought we were trying to poach. Under the new system this difficulty has vanished because we now have no children who belong to other churches.

After all this closing down and tightening up, I began to assess the needs of the parish with a view to starting other organizations and to look out for potential leaders. First we started a branch of the Church of England Men's Society, and we publicly enrolled thirty men just before the Family Communion. A Young Wives Fellowship quickly followed. A company of the Church Lads' Brigade, sponsored and run by members of the C.E.M.S., came next, to cater for the needs of boys who were not attracted to Scouting, and a branch of the Girls' Friendly Society, sponsored by the Mothers' Union, followed in due course.

We are a great church for sport, and we have our own sports clubs now. One of the great problems in our big cities is that young people are content just to watch others play games, and big numbers of teenagers watch professional football, not realizing that it is much more fun and much better for you to play something yourself. We started our own Badminton Club first, in a much lower league, of course, than its distinguished predecessor but confined to our own people. A football team came next, and now we have two teams playing in the local leagues, and there is keen competition to play. We have a Cricket Club and a Tennis Club. Suitable playing fields are not in very good supply, but we found the local education committee most helpful, and they provide us with all we need at remarkably low charges. A Youth Club, meeting after Evensong on Sunday nights and on one week-night as well, completed the organizations strictly confined to existing church members.

It is essential to have a clear strategy in mind when planning clubs and organizations for young people. The old way was to make all members attend a special Bible Class on Sunday afternoons, and membership of the club was conditional on this obligation being fulfilled. It never really worked. This was the Portsea pattern so ably described by Canon Charles Smyth in his *Life of Garbett* (page 106): 'But, as the clergy themselves were very conscious, there was always the danger of "Club Christianity," with members drifting away from the church when they ceased to belong to the club, and even, while they still belonged to it, making the Bible Class a substitute for church attendance. Viewed in retrospect, the clubs are apt to appear a doubtful and a wasting asset.' This method was given the soundest and most practical application by the members of a brilliant staff at Portsea, and we can say that if it did not work there and in those conditions, it is unlikely to work anywhere —if by 'work' you mean build up the young people of the parish into instructed and committed adult worshippers. And nothing less will do.

Yet this method did some good. It at least led to good-will for the church. Not even this can be said for the more up-to-date method of the church running clubs for all and sundry without any obligations involving church attendance, where the pious hope is that some will be drawn via the club into the church when they see what good types the churchgoing minority really are. It is possible that the reverse may be achieved. It is possible that the churchgoing minority may be led away from the church by the noisy majority. If you put a few canaries into a cage with a lot of sparrows with the idea of getting the canaries to teach the sparrows to sing you sould not be too surprised if you find that the sparrows have taught the canaries to chirp.

Our way works. The clubs are not drag nets. The way into them is via the church, and they are only open to those who accept the obligation of attendance at the chief service of the day. Nobody feels that they are being 'got at' and there is no resentment worth talking about because newcomers know exactly where they stand. But it is vital that the obligation should be to attend an adult service and not something specially laid on for young people. This overcomes the difficulty of the youngster leaving the club and the church, and we have many who left the club long ago, but who are still faithful weekly communicants. But the adult service must be bright and lively. To make attendance compulsory at a dull and turgid one would be unpardonable.

All the organizations had to be run by lay people and not by the clergy. I was lucky enough to secure the services of a first rate assistant curate after I had been here a few months, but I had to make it clear that neither he nor I would be available to run any organizations in the evenings because we had visiting and all sorts of other things to do. We would look in, and we would talk and instruct and help, but we could not be more heavily involved than that.

All these organizations were strictly confined to our own people, and I told the leaders that one of the rules for everybody had to be attendance every Sunday at the Family Communion, and those not willing to accept this simple obligation should be asked to leave. I told them that there was a deeper object than teaching the tying of knots or gymnastics or scoring goals. We were going to try to build up integrated personalities and produce men and women of upright principles and sound outlook. As part of all this, religion was to play a prominent part, and I made it clear that I looked to each organization to produce a steady stream of confirmation candidates. The clergy would help, but leadership, I told them, involved leadership of this kind.

c*

I have been fortunate in my leaders, both in those I found here when I came and in those who have since come forward. They know what is expected of them, and they have carried out loyally and efficiently the policy laid down. The final picture is not as neat and tidy as one could wish, and the rules are not kept with unvarying strictness. Not all the members, not even all the leaders, are present every Sunday morning. But most of them are. All members have the claims of Jesus Christ brought before them. Most of them know and respect and value the Sunday morning service and the organizations do, in fact, produce that steady stream of confirmation candidates that I wanted to see. Those who come to me in this way are nearly always of excellent quality, and it is not the members of organizations who drift away afterwards. They are the ones who remain faithful because they are heavily involved at the outset.

It was also clear that we must provide some things of a light social nature, because if we did not provide them nobody else would. It was decided that well-run dances should be held regularly, and we started an Old Time Dancing Class that was an instant success, and a whist drive for older folk.

These things were so new to Ambrosians that I had to make it very clear that they were perfectly harmless. I wrote this in the magazine soon after my arrival:

Whist Drives and Dances—these things are new to St. Ambrose folk, and I expect I am right in assuming that some of our people regard them as wrong.

It is important to know just why we think some things are wrong. The reasons why some regard cards and dancing as coming under this heading are usually as follows:

1. Because they are wrong in themselves.

2. Because they are wrong on church property, which should be used for more serious purposes, have no connection with the preaching of the Gospel, and encourage flippancy.

3. Because it is wrong to raise money for church upkeep by such indirect methods, and people should be taught that

there is no substitute for the direct sacrificial giving that being a Christian involves.

Let's look at these points. No. 1 can be quickly dismissed. Very few things are wrong in themselves, although they can become wrong through excess or misuse. Things like murder, adultery, stealing and lying are obviously wrong in themselves and can never be any other. They outrage the human conscience, transgress the known will of God, and are expressly condemned by the Ten Commandments. Christians have always known these things to be wrong and there are other things, once lightly considered, that we now do not hesitate to condemn as wrong in themselves—the colour bar, for instance, and cruelty to animals. We believe these things to be contrary to the teaching of Jesus and offensive to enlightened Christian opinion. They are worth getting heated about. But it would be ludicrous to condemn recreations such as we are considering on these grounds.

No. 2 merits more careful consideration. The Puritans were responsible for bringing into church life an atmosphere of sustained gloom, but this atmosphere is not necessarily a sign of intense devotion to our Lord, and I find it hard to reconcile with the story of the marriage feast at Cana. There is nothing in the Gospels that condemns innocent laughter and wholesome recreation. After all, Christians should be the happiest of people. They have something to be happy about. It is entirely fitting that people who worship together Sunday by Sunday should find their recreations and amusements more worthwhile and more enjoyable in the company of their fellow Christians, and we seek to provide for those who take this view.

No. 3, however, is an objection that I fully share. It is an appalling state of affairs when a church relies on whist drives and dances for the money needed to keep the church going, and I would like to emphasize that money raising by these means should be regarded as purely secondary. The chief purpose is to promote friendliness and social intercourse. For the upkeep of the church we rely on the direct giving of the congregation, and I ask all who share this view loyally to support the Freewill Offering Envelope scheme, which is the corner stone of our whole financial edifice, and which makes less worthy methods of money-raising unnecessary.

Meanwhile, we want tolerance, understanding and criticism of self rather than of others. If you have been brought up to regard whist drives and dancing as wrong, I ask you to revise your opinions in the light of what I have written, and consider what Paul meant when he spoke of being all things to all men with the single object of winning some for Christ. If you regard such disapproval as narrow and out-of-date, then remember that those who hold these views are no less sincere than you are, and their devotion to their Master and their church is often beyond praise.

There were no very loud objections, and soon we had these things running regularly. What an asset that small hall soon proved to be! Once the billiards tables were out we could make full use of it, and it was not long before both halls were in use practically every night. In the light of experience we made the whist drives and dances open to everybody, at the request of those who came and who wanted to bring along friends and neighbours. Quite a few strangers began to come regularly, and some still do, but it may be worth putting on record that I do not think we have gained one single church member who has come in through any social occasion. The theory that these open things first of all bring people into the hall and then into the church simply does not work out. Organizations that are meant to be drag nets are usually most disappointing.

In 1959 we reorganized and greatly improved the Sunday Night Youth Club by dividing it into two sections—a senior section for those over fifteen and a junior section for those under fifteen—meeting in separate halls with separate committees, subscriptions, and leaders. Each has a varied programme covering different tastes, but the senior club has a programme that differs markedly from that thought suitable for the juniors. The emphasis is on doing things, and talks and discussions and preparation for responsible adult church membership.

A great feature is the 'Black Hand Gang' who undertake jobs such as gardening or decorating for house-bound old-age pensioners. 'Rock and roll' is absolutely banned on Sunday nights for both sections, not because we think it is wrong, but because a full programme makes this sort of thing superfluous. The seniors meet on Tuesdays for games and lighter activities, and those who want their 'bopping' (horrible word!) can have it then. Nearly a hundred of our teenagers come regularly to this club on Sunday evenings.

The one absolute rule for all members is attendance at Family Communion. If this rule was relaxed we could probably get far greater numbers—and the result would be utter chaos. There is a tremendous demand for something to do on Sunday nights by young people in our great cities, but we feel here that we can only meet the needs of committed church members. Our young people do in fact bring their friends to Family Communion so that they can qualify for club membership, and some have been brought into full membership of the church by this means. It is certain that the Family Communion is a converting influence. It may be worth recording that fifty teenagers were confirmed in 1960, youngsters of excellent quality who seem deeply interested, a far greater number than we have ever had before.

It will be seen that the key people in all the above are lay folk who are willing to do things with devotion and a clear aim, and it is to this subject that we must now turn.

CHAPTER SEVEN

ENLISTING LAY SUPPORT

ONE man said to me in my first week here: 'Vicar, I want to warn you about your P.C.C. They are a two-faced lot. They will say one thing to your face, and another behind your back. Don't trust them an inch because they will let you down.' Another man said to me the same week: 'You have a wonderful lot of people here. They are devoted to their church and are ready for anything. Tell them all you have in mind for the parish, take them into your confidence, and you will not find a better lot of workers in all Bristol.' I need not say who was right! Clearly the help and general co-operation of the people was going to be necessary because the parish contained 1,772 houses, and the population was stated to be about 6,000 people by the 1951 census; and this makes quite a lot of people. Without lay help and lots of it my job was going to be a nightmare.

I wanted at least one representative in every street. The forty magazine distributors, good church people all, were the obvious ones to appoint, and the first thing to do was to get each distributor to do his or her street and no other. This meant breaking up rounds that had been established for years, and required careful handling. An outstanding magazine secretary proved her worth here by personally calling on each distributor shortly after I had outlined the scheme in church, and she managed to persuade each one to fall in with the new idea with no friction of any kind. And so the Waywardens organization was born. The name caught my eye in a magazine article, and it seemed to me to be an admirable term to describe the people and job, as I explained in a letter that was distributed to every house in the parish:

Dear Parishioner,

ST. AMBROSE WAYWARDENS

In wartime the street wardens were regarded as friends and helpers. The Christian religion was first called 'The Way.' This explains our Waywardens scheme and I want to tell you something about it.

We are trying to appoint somebody in every street in the parish who will represent the church. We call them Waywardens and they are asked to let the clergy know of all cases of serious illness, accidents, those going to hospital, deaths, etc., except where the person concerned is a member of another denomination and looked after by another minister. Please send for us if you have any problems, worries or queries where you think we may be able to help.

Waywardens are also asked to distribute the parish magazine, display window bills, and give any information they can about the church and its services and organizations. The more you make use of them the better pleased they will be.

For your street the Waywarden is.......... of..........

It did not take long to get one established in most of the streets, although it proved impossible in some just because we had no church member whatsoever living there. In this case the representative of a neighbouring street was asked to look after both. Each Waywarden was given a small but attractively designed card to display in the window, with the words 'St. Ambrose Waywarden' surrounding an impression of the church. In addition to the duties outlined in the letter they were also asked to distribute letters from me from time to time, some to the church members only, and some to every house, and they were also asked to display posters announcing various church events.

Some Waywardens do their job well. One excellent result is that the clergy are now on the scene in good time. We know that people should send for the clergy as readily as they do for the doctor when they need our ministrations—but they just don't! Now we get there when we can still do some good. They have brought new people to church and introduced them to us, they have been responsible for new children coming to Sunday school, they have helped people in trouble who have turned naturally and readily to them, including those with no church affiliations of any kind. Incidentally they have pushed up the circulation of the magazine from 285 copies a month to well over 500, and one outstanding person enrolled every householder in her street, all twenty-six of them, as subscribers.

All Waywardens were given a bulk supply of forms which they were asked to fill in and bring with them every Sunday morning, and this proved to be a much tidier arrangement than the odd bits of paper that used to come along. These forms are simple enough:

WAYWARDEN'S RETURN FOR WEEK ENDING.....
LIST FOR .... STREET
ANY SICK ....
ANY DEATHS...............................
ANY NEWCOMERS ....
VISITS FOR SPECIAL REASONS ....
                    (*Signed*)................

The whole scheme began splendidly, but the usual difficulties were experienced as the years went on. Some faithful ones never failed us, but the enthusiasm of some others began to dwindle, and they became rather slack and careless. It became necessary to reorganize the whole scheme, and this was done in 1959. We now have forty-five Waywardens divided into eight areas, each with an area-secretary, with one general secretary in charge of them all. All reports are brought to the Family Communion and collected by the general secretary and handed to the vicar for consideration and action at the Tuesday staff meeting.

The Parochial Church Council had to be used thoroughly. Members should be the cream of the parish, elected because of their capacity to plan and carry out work in collaboration with the incumbent both within and beyond the parish, but I found meetings at first tended to be dreary and rather lengthy affairs, devoted mostly to finance in one form or another. It was clear that a change of procedure had to be made. We increased the membership from thirty to forty, and formed committees. Most members were familiar with the procedure of the local City Council, where the real work is done by the committees and brought before the full council for brief discussion and approval or otherwise, and we decided to follow this pattern. We formed Finance, Evangelistic, Church Buildings, Missionary, Social and Catering committees, each to meet once a quarter before the meeting of the full council.

This procedure makes the meetings of the full council much more stimulating. We do not waste time endlessly discussing comparatively trivial things because all these have been thoroughly considered in committee. It is rare for a committee resolution to be turned down, and exceptional for it to be referred back. At the full council meetings we can take some really big theme and consider it together without desperately hurrying on to the next point. I have kept my original undertaking, and nothing of any real importance has been introduced without prior discussion with the P.C.C.

The Finance Committee has had the toughest assignment because money raising in a working-class parish is harder than in others. Working-class churches have for years been on the receiving end, and the folk have not until recently had much to give and have not been taught to give. Now things are different. Wages are high. They spend very freely on consumer goods, but giving to the church is not generally very good apart from the few who support everything. There are some who do give and give very generously, but it just does not occur to many who earn good money to give sacrificially, and this is specially true of young people. My churchwarden told me that he noticed three young men in church not long ago, all of whom were in work. One put 3*d*. in the collection plate, one nothing at all, and one a ½*d*.! I do not suggest that this is general, but it is true that our working-class folk can well afford to be much more generous than in fact they are, and money raising has thus been a headache throughout my incumbency.

I have before me a sermon I preached at the Parish Communion in my second year here. It was on Whitsunday, a day when I could be sure of having practically every regular member present, and the theme was 'Grant us by the same Spirit to have a right judgement in all things.' This is what I had to say about giving:

Now what about our own church? God has blessed us. We have prayed and prayed for the guidance of the Holy Spirit and everything that has happened here has been conceived in prayer. The little Saturday evening prayer meeting has been of the utmost help and this lovely service in which we are now sharing is one of the fruits. It is good to see so many of you here, older folk, families, young people, children. We have splendid organizations with devoted leaders and everything is going well.

I should have said 'nearly everything,' for one thing is missing. Last Wednesday we had a rather gloomy meeting of the Finance Committee, when an overdraft of £150 on the general account was reported by the treasurer. We are almost certainly going to end the year with a big overdraft unless something is done, because the plain fact is that our expenditure exceeds our income. We have to study everything very carefully, and we have to cut down where we ought to increase, because prices are going up all the time and our income is not.

Here is the one thing missing. There were fifty three halfcrowns in the collection last Sunday. Sixpence is still the commonest coin. Only about fifty people give really sacrificially here, and they give until it hurts. They are the ones who put most on the collection plate, and the same ones give most generously in their C.M.S. boxes and support every special effort and every special appeal. But what about the rest of you? Those of you who are earning and who give

6*d*. or 3*d*. or even less are simply not doing your stuff, and some of you young people especially seem to want everything here on the cheap.

We are held up at every turn by this fact, and the stranglehold of constant nagging worry about money is more likely than anything else to kill stone dead all that you and I are seeking to do for God.

We have everything here but this. What are you going to do about it? Let's be practical. Will some of you try to double your contributions? If you want a standard, what about giving each Sunday the amount you earn in one hour? Many people are adopting some such standard, and it is a reasonable one that should not be impossible for most of you.

You see you are the very heart of St. Ambrose. I could not preach this sermon at Evensong. You are the ones. Pray about this and see where the Holy Spirit leads you. Put this one thing right and we can go right ahead. At present I believe this to be the thing that most grieves the Holy Spirit of God—this general unwillingness of St. Ambrose folk (all but fifty or so) to pay up.

This was not the first appeal for money, indeed many more moderately worded ones had been made, including the annual appeal for more members of the Freewill Offering Envelope scheme. They did not have much effect. It is true that our collections were going steadily up, but this was because our numbers were increasing and not because more sacrificial standards were being accepted. The members of the Finance Committee put it to me that it was not really my job, and suggested that lay people could probably do it better, a suggestion with which I found myself in entire agreement. Towards the end of 1956 they got to work. The vicar's warden addressed the congregation in church before the Family Communion, and outlined a new system of family giving, i.e. a family having one communal envelope to put in weekly. Charts were prepared by the treasurer and displayed, and members of the Finance Committee addressed our youth organizations and answered questions. The job was done thoroughly and the response was immediate, so that our collections for 1957 went up very sharply.

Here are the figures:

Year			Total collections
1953	..	..	£519
1954	..	..	£697
1955	..	..	£912
1956	..	..	£986
1957	..	..	£1,223
1958	..	..	£1,198
1959	..	..	£2,145

This new weekly average of a little over £20 enabled us to pay our way, but only just—and we were always slightly in the red. We gave about £170 to the Church Missionary Society, and paid our quota of £240 in full, but it was obvious that our collections had settled down to about £20 a week and we had to face the alternatives of putting up with this or doing something drastic and really challenging. We decided to call in the professionals and to give them a hearing. In 1958 we had the first professionally directed fund-raising campaign in the Bristol diocese, and this campaign, run by laymen for laymen, will be described in detail in the next chapter.

The ancient office of churchwarden provides a wonderful field for lay service. What a mistake it is for churchwardens to remain in office for very long periods. They think as year follows year and they are re-elected each time, that nobody else is willing to serve, and if a life sentence is involved they are probably right. I told my P.C.C. when I first came that I thought two years in office was enough. The Lord Mayor of Bristol can only serve for one year, and I quoted this as showing the desirability of this, the highest elected office the church has to offer, going the rounds. The P.C.C. agreed with this idea, but we could not make it a rule. Anybody can be elected by the Easter Vestry Meeting. In fact the system has worked well, and we now elect a new one each year who serves his first year as people's warden, the junior office, and his second as vicar's warden. There is never any difficulty in getting suitable people to be nominated, and the yearly ballot means we get the people who are really wanted. Already I have nine men who have served or who are serving in this capacity and who thus have an intimate knowledge of every aspect of the work. Church-wardens are *ex-officio* members of every committee, and during their two years of service the demands made upon them are considerable. After they have been sworn in at the Archdeacon's Visitation they are solemnly admitted to their office just before the Family Communion and given their wands.

This constant changing of churchwardens is wholly good. Each year we think we shall never get a man as good as the one recently retired, but we always do. They attend nearly all the committee meetings and most church functions, and they take their duties very seriously indeed. They take charge of a team of thirty sidesmen, supervise the communicants at the Family Communion, cope with people who feel ill, and spend a great deal of time on weekdays as well as Sundays in helping forward the work of the church.

The churchwardens' wives enjoy tremendously their two years of reflected glory. Women who have remained quietly in the background for years find themselves brought right into the foreground and grow in stature in the most surprising way. They sit on the platform on the various big occasions, and become capable of taking a leading part in the various organizations. They remain most valuable assets after the two years are over.

The churchwardens have specially constructed raised seats at the back of the church, and these help to make clear the dignity and importance of the office. To make fuller use of these men I have formed them into a body of elders, spelt with a small 'e' to avoid question begging. The idea has sound New Testament authority, and the idea is familiar to those who know anything about the

Presbyterian system of Church government, but I had in mind something much less formal, as the letter sent to each of these indicates:

I have had it in my mind for some time that lay people should have a greater say in the affairs of St. Ambrose Church. Here at St. Ambrose we are very fortunate in having a number of men with great experience in the running of the parish because they are serving or have served in the office of church-warden.

One of the fruits of our plan here that the churchwardens only remain in office for two years is that we now have no less than eight men in the congregation who have had this valuable experience.

I would very much like to have a body of elders here, made up of churchwardens and ex-churchwardens and nobody else. The idea would not be to side-track the P.C.C. or to conflict with it in any way. I have in mind an advisory body that would help me to sort out matters that are always considered to be the vicar's prerogative and his alone, i.e. the ordering of services, the inviting of visiting preachers, the preparation of confirmation candidates, the training of assistant curates and the making of appointments. These are not the sort of things that are dealt with by the P.C.C. but by the vicar alone. It is here that I would be grateful for your assistance.

The purpose of this letter is to invite you to come to a meeting in the Committee Room next Sunday at 11.30 a.m. when we can explore the possibilities.

The meeting was duly held and the project accepted. Since then the elders have proved their worth. One of the best things they do is to take one confirmation class of boys and girls in my absence. One man speaks to them about the sort of problems they may expect to be confronted with when they leave school and start work, another says something about his own Confirmation, a third, licensed by the bishop to administer the chalice, tells them what he really feels when he does so. All of them answer questions afterwards and a most successful class it is, one that makes a very deep impression on the candidates.

Lay people can be a great help with secretarial work too. What a lot of time we spend on this in a busy parish! One of the first things I had made here was a parish office, and we managed to acquire a second-hand electric duplicator and typewriter. I asked for volunteers to help with the typing and duplicating, and we got three, all experts, who made this their own church work, one making herself responsible for my own personal work, and the other two for the parish matters. They have given most valuable service.

It seemed to me at the outset here that I must get lay people to do the things I had previously done myself, and thus leave myself free to get on with the real job of a priest. If the incumbent tries to do himself all the things that lay folk can do as well, then something has to go by the board, and that is usually something vital. The truth is that lay folk can do certain things a great deal better than we can, and they grow in grace in the doing of them.

CHAPTER EIGHT

A PROFESSIONAL FUND-RAISING CAMPAIGN

I HAVE said that we employed a professional fund-raising organization to put our finances in order. Most people know about these organizations now, but they were comparatively unknown early in 1958, and our Finance Committee was rather against employing them because it seemed to be wrong in principle. The point is not really a valid one because we do not hesitate to employ lawyers and architects and heating specialists and all sorts of other experts in their professional capacities, indeed we are encouraged to ask and pay for the best professional advice and not to leave important things to willing but not very competent volunteers. The plain fact was that we were in difficulties, and could see no other way out of them and thus, with some misgivings, we wrote to the Wells Organization and asked them to send a representative to meet us.

A date was fixed, and a very able man arrived from London and spent the afternoon with me, going fully into the parish statistics, before meeting the Finance Committee in the evening. He wanted to see last year's balance sheet to find out the previous direct giving. He wanted to know how many names were on the Electoral Roll, how many Easter communicants, how many in the Sunday school and the Youth Organizations, how many weddings and baptisms there had been. He wanted to know how many families we could look to for support and how much our total needs really were for the next three years. It was agreed that our existing direct giving was £26 per week (including collections, missionary boxes, and donations) and that we wanted to raise this to about £46 to cover all existing commitments and to double our support for the Church Missionary Society. He said that this was reasonable and possible, and offered to sign a contract guaranteeing to raise collections to this figure. This campaign would cover 200 families, last three weeks, and would cost £750 in fee investment (paid in instalments) and £250 campaign expenses.

The Finance Committee had many questions to ask. What would happen in those three weeks? What methods would be used to secure such astonishing results? How would he succeed where we had failed? If all giving was to be direct, what would happen to money-raising efforts such as fêtes and bazaars, which were eagerly looked forward to as social occasions? The answers were plain enough. We were told that a Campaign Director would arrive, and would expect to find a properly equipped office complete with shorthand-typist, telephone, typewriter and adding machine, and he would also expect to be given a complete list of the 200 families in alphabetical order, with a list of twenty or so leading laymen who could give generously. His first jobs would be to arrange a big Loyalty Dinner and to arrange for the publication of an elaborate illustrated brochure to be sent to all. He would get into personal contact with the twenty men, teach them the principles of Christian giving, and get as many as possible of them to sign pledges for generous amounts. It would be their job to visit all the other families and get them to sign pledges too. He told us that although fêtes and bazaars would no longer be necessary for church fund-raising, yet they could still be held as social occasions, provided that the proceeds were given to outside objects. The Finance Committee was convinced that the strategy and methods outlined were soundly Christian and, after several meetings lasting many hours, a unanimous recommendation was made to the Parochial Church Council to have a campaign.

Two meetings of the Parochial Church Council (one addressed by the Wells spokesman) were held and more difficulties were raised. It was said that our men would never agree to do the visiting, and anyway, nobody could spare the time required. It was pointed out that our people were very touchy about money matters and would never disclose the amount they were prepared to give. It was stressed that wage packets in this parish were lower than in most others, and the threat of unemployment was a very real one. The Wells spokesman dealt with all these objections, and communicated his own optimism to the meeting. Eventually it was resolved that we would have the campaign provided that the bank manager would provide overdraft facilities to meet the very heavy expenses and this, after reference to his head office and on the strength of the Wells guarantee, he agreed to do. This guarantee stated clearly that in twelve months the new giving would equal the old direct giving plus the total cost of the campaign, and if there was a deficit it would be met by the Wells Organization.

We began in October 1958. A highly competent Campaign Director arrived full of energy and enthusiasm, and himself a dedicated Christian. A handsome brochure was produced very quickly and distributed. A team of women hostesses was organized, and they personally approached all our families with an invitation to attend the dinner. The dinner took place in the second week and was a tremendous occasion, with 200 people attending. Meanwhile the leading members of the congregation had been seen personally and most of them entered wholeheartedly into the campaign and signed pledges for amazingly generous amounts from £1 a week downwards. Several of these were trained to make speeches at the dinner, outlining and explaining the whole campaign.

After the dinner the visiting began. The list of families had grown from 200 to 277, and eighteen men agreed to visit the lot, and this was done in the course of the next fortnight. Of course they dreaded it. They expected to be greeted with hostility, but in the event their fears proved to be groundless. Almost without exception they received a warm welcome, and as they came back to the office to report progress, night after night, so their enthusiasm mounted. Of course the ground had been thoroughly prepared by the brochure and the dinner, and it was only church members that were called on. The visitors made many new friends, and a typical comment afterwards was: 'I wouldn't have missed it for anything.' In the end 156 families signed pledges amounting to £35 per week.

The first meeting of the Continuation Committee was held six weeks after the beginning of the new system of giving, and it was found that collections during these six weeks had averaged £38 per week compared with £19 for a similar period the previous year. Nearly everybody who signed pledges had faithfully carried out their voluntary obligations. After six months collections had risen to an average of £41 a Sunday.

It must be recognized that certain difficulties appear when you have a campaign of this nature. You do not enter Satan's stronghold without getting a buffeting. For instance, we very soon discovered that we were not as unanimous as we had supposed, and some of our leading laymen who voted for the scheme at the Parochial Church Council meeting decided, after we were fully committed, to contract out, and inevitably the parish was divided. This division tended to increase as the campaign went on, and those who signed very generous pledges had some hard things to say about those who did not. Why did some refuse to pledge? The Wells people have a wonderfully expressive phrase—'Pocket Book Protection'! It is self-explanatory and is probably somewhere near the truth. But people are not all alike, and some refused to change their convictions and preferred to stay out. It would be lovely to be able to record that we had a completely united team effort, that we met with a completely unanimous response, but this was not the case.

It has taken a long time and much hard work to re-establish the unity of the parish. Another difficulty that ought to be mentioned is that if you do the whole thing on a bank overdraft you are in the discouraging position of having a very big income coming in and no money available for anything until it is paid off.

I was amazed at the generosity of those who pledged. This is a working-class parish, and many of our people earn very modest wage packets. They were told that the standard to be aimed at should be the Biblical tithe—one-tenth of income taken home to be given to God, and quite a few decided to do just that. Four families pledged £1 a week, and a large number 10s. Two families with less than £9 coming in pledged 7s. 6d. each. Old-age pensioners were asked for nothing, but many insisted on coming in and signed for up to 2s. 6d. a week. A girl who had just left school promised 3s., and a boy 4s. One woman, whose husband never comes to church, said to her visitor: 'Let me sign for 2s. before my husband comes home.' The visitor rightly refused to accept this pledge and insisted that her husband should first be consulted. He called the following evening and met the husband, who insisted that the 2s. should be increased to 4s. The average actually given works out at approximately 4s. 6d. per week per family.

The follow-up is all important. Families leave the parish. People die. We have to be constantly on the look out for new members. We had a leaflet printed that runs as follows:

You must have noticed that many of our families put one envelope between them into the collection plate. This is because we have the planned giving system here. THIS MEANS THAT OUR MEMBERS HAVE BEEN ASKED TO THINK OUT WHAT THEIR CHURCH MEANS TO THEM AND TO SET ASIDE WEEKLY AN AMOUNT WHICH REPRESENTS GENUINE SACRIFICE. MANY OF THEM HAVE DONE THIS AND THOSE WHO 'PASS THE PLATE' ARE PROBABLY MEMBERS OF SUCH FAMILIES AND THUS AMONGST OUR MOST GENEROUS SUPPORTERS.

We no longer have all sorts of indirect money-raising events to support this church. It is all done by the direct giving of families who love this place or who feel they owe something to it. We hope that in time we shall be able to give much more away; for instance, to the Bishop's Development Appeal (for churches in new housing estates) and to the Church overseas. There is no limit to the amount of help that can be given to others in need of help.

ALL WHO COME HERE REGULARLY OR WHO REGARD ST. AMBROSE AS THEIR CHURCH ARE ASKED TO CONSIDER JOINING THE SCHEME. THOSE WHO WOULD LIKE MORE INFORMATION SHOULD FILL IN THEIR NAMES AND ADDRESSES AND GIVE THE ENCLOSED PAPER TO ONE OF THE WARDENS—OR SIMPLY TELL HIM. ONE OF OUR LAYMEN WILL THEN CALL WITH FULL DETAILS.

You may feel you would like some information about one or other of our organizations, either for yourself or for your children. If so, a tick against the ones in which you are interested will bring you the required information. AND WHAT ABOUT HAVING THE MAGAZINE BROUGHT TO YOUR DOOR EACH MONTH?

A large notice has been posted in a prominent position in the porch with the following wording:

THE PLANNED GIVING SYSTEM

OPERATES IN THIS CHURCH. FAMILIES HAVE UNDERTAKEN TO PUT A FIXED WEEKLY AMOUNT (IN ONE ENVELOPE) INTO THE COLLECTION AND ONE MEMBER OF EACH FAMILY PUTS THE ENVELOPE IN AT ONE SERVICE. THUS THOSE WHO 'PASS THE PLATE' ARE PROBABLY OUR MOST GENEROUS SUPPORTERS. WE HAVE NO MONEY-RAISING EFFORTS FOR CHURCH EXPENSES OR UPKEEP. EVERYTHING DEPENDS ON PLANNED GIVING. THOSE WHO WOULD LIKE DETAILS OF THE SCHEME SHOULD ASK ONE OF THE WARDENS.

It is encouraging to note that as the months go on the amount contributed week by week has tended to increase rather than to decrease, although several people, including some of the biggest pledgers, have already left the parish.

At the time of writing we have ended our first year of pledged giving and collections, totalling £2,145, exceed those of the previous year by £947. The vast majority of those who signed pledges have faithfully kept their undertaking, particularly those who pledged large amounts. It is those who pledged comparatively small amounts that have dropped out, including a number of teenagers.

We have had our 'Follow-up Canvass' and new members have been visited by our men as well as old members who previously refused to join. Two of our leading opponents to the scheme have changed their minds in the light of experience, and have decided to join in, and we have nineteen new pledges signed. Our men mean to keep this scheme going because it is so absolutely right. It is wonderful to feel that practically all members are helping to share the load, and to know that events such as fêtes and bazaars are largely social affairs with the money-raising purely secondary and always for some worthy outside object.

We have a 'Junior Wells Campaign' planned for the near future,[1] one specially for teenagers following the pattern set for the adults. The Youth Club is going to run it, and is drawing up a list of all teenagers with any connections with the church. The Parochial Church Council is providing £20 for a Loyalty Dinner that will be held for them in the Church Hall, with our own people doing the catering, and for the necessary duplicating. Teenage speakers are being trained to launch the campaign and a team of them is going to make a personal approach to all the others inviting them to sign pledge cards.

It will be a separate scheme from the main one in that our young people will keep the records themselves, and go after those who get behind in their payments. It is early days yet to say whether this will succeed, but my opinion is that it will, and if it does it will succeed where all other

[1] This Campaign was actually held in May 1960 (between the writing and publication of this book), when 97 teenagers signed pledges for generous amounts totalling about £5 10s. weekly and 21 others decided to remain in the original family scheme.

approaches have failed. Our young people are not good
at giving, and this is certainly not because they are short
of money.

Certain facts stand out a mile. These professional
fund-raisers know exactly what they are doing, and are
able to perform the seemingly impossible. Their methods
are wholly Christian, and we saw nothing of transatlantic
slickness or sensationalism. The appeal is for genuine
sacrificial giving to God, and the whole method is based
on a personal approach. One interesting thing that I
noticed was that when people give generously the desire
for secrecy goes completely.

One effect of a campaign of this nature is that the full
responsibility for fund-raising is placed firmly on the
shoulders of the laymen of the parish, where it ought to be.
Our laymen do this job far more competently than we
clergy can ever hope to do. The Parochial Church Council
ought now to be able to concentrate on the really vital
job of extending the kingdom of Jesus Christ within and
without the parish.

I feel sure that the method of planned giving with an
every member canvass will become as general in England
as it already is in the Commonwealth and in America.
The method really works, and it can be adapted for any
type of parish, quite regardless of the needs of that parish.
The whole point about such a campaign is simply the
need of the giver to give. These professionals lay down
that every parish ought to give away at least as much as
it spends on itself, and if we got anywhere near such a
standard the whole picture would be transformed. The
Central Board of Finance of the Church of England, in
its excellent booklet, *The Christian Stewardship of Money*,
makes it abundantly plain that something has to be
done. Is it generally known that in 1956 only 47 per cent
of the income of Parochial Church Councils was produced
by direct giving, and the remaining 53 per cent by 'special
efforts' that include bazaars, fêtes, sales of work, jumble

sales, and so on? The average giving, direct and indirect, represented 2s. 7d. weekly per Easter communicant. These figures are really appalling, and the work of the whole Church of England has been gravely hindered as a result.

These professionals have shown us very clearly that the problem is not insoluble. We have got to learn from them. It seems to me that the Church of England ought to set up its own fund-raising organization, and I look forward to the day when every diocese or group of dioceses has its own full time organizer who would conduct campaigns in any parish for a much smaller fee than is at present charged. It does not require supermen to do this important work. It simply requires dedicated Christian men who have undergone a short period of training and who have been involved in several campaigns under expert direction. It ought not to be difficult to find men who would regard such a job as well worth doing. I would like to see them stress the fact that giving is a spiritual matter, and that it is not one-tenth but ten-tenths of all that we have and all that we are that belongs to God. Real stewardship involves far more than the giving of money, but the sacrificial giving of money is an essential part of stewardship.

CHAPTER NINE

CHILDREN AND YOUNG PEOPLE

I SAID earlier that we have six schools in this parish. There is a Mixed Infant school that my daughter attended for the usual two years, and a Junior school that she also attended. There is a very big Grammar school for boys and girls, and another for girls only, and we also have two Secondary Modern schools, one for boys and one for girls, that have recently become Bilateral, i.e. they have a number of Grammar school standard pupils as well. They are all run by the Local Education Authority.

I find myself a welcome visitor in all of them. I am allowed to walk around the class rooms, and to meet both children and staff, and to find out what is being taught. The Heads of these schools are all of them close friends and I have had many talks with all of them. They invite me to school events, and I make a point of going to as many as possible. In one I am a member of the Board of Governors. Religion counts for a great deal in these schools, and I find that Scripture is taught extremely well and the daily act of worship reverently conducted. They make good use of their parish church. They have special Christmas Carol Services here, and these services are always an inspiration. From time to time special services are held, e.g. on Ash Wednesday and Ascension Day, and at the end of term. I am sometimes invited to take part in services in the schools themselves.

What a wonderful opportunity we have in these state schools! It is a great mistake to suppose that there is any hostility to the Church of England. The contrary is true, and I find that any help I can give is welcomed. The Heads and members of the staff often prove to be keen and convinced church members themselves, and the

D   97

proportion is sufficiently high to reflect great credit on our excellent Church Training Colleges. Our state schools have never been better. I do not really regret that we have no Church school in the parish. If I wanted to give denominational teaching in these state schools, and if the parents wanted this, then it could easily be arranged by having 'withdrawal' classes that our children could attend in school hours, and taken by me. But I have done nothing about this. Surely denominational teaching has very little value unless it is linked with membership of the church family, and the ideal place to forge these links is in the parish church itself. The schools teach all sorts of things, including religious knowledge, extremely well. But there are certain things that I do not believe can be taught in school, and one of them is personal religion and the feeling of belonging to a worshipping congregation. This cannot be taught in a day school, not even in a Church school, and opportunities must thus be made for teaching the children on Sundays in church and on weekdays in their church organizations.

Of course a good Church school is a very great asset, and it is good to know that recent government legislation has made it possible to retain some and thus to give the Church a more definite say in the educational policy of the country. But those parishes that feel they simply cannot manage the 25 per cent of the cost of rebuilding need not feel that anything of supreme value has been irrecoverably lost. It is possible to work in closely with state schools if the incumbent is found to be tactful and interested in the work that they do.

The strategy is plain enough here. My job, it seemed to me, was to make good use of the opportunities provided by the state schools, and then to make further opportunities in my parish for teaching the children and young people who were actual or potential members of the church, and leading them farther. Teaching, imparting information, is vitally important, but it is not the most vital thing of all. The most vital thing is to lead the youngsters to the making of a decision. I wanted to lead them to Christ, to help them to decide to accept full membership of the Church with its privileges and its responsibilities. I did not want diffused good-will. I did not want just attendance at church services. I wanted decisions leading to Confirmation and then beyond Confirmation to sanctification, and our parochial machinery had to be overhauled with this in mind.

The Sunday school was rather small, but well staffed by a small number of keen teachers. It soon began to grow when the new policy for our organizations came into operation. As I have already said, membership of the Scouts and Cubs, Guides and Brownies, Girls' Friendly Society, and Church Lads' Brigade became available only to church members, and this was assumed to involve attending afternoon Sunday school. The numbers soon went up from about 150 to about 250, and we had no difficulty in enrolling new teachers. My curate took over the Sunday school and made it one of his chief jobs, and it is now a very good one. The teachers come to his preparation classes and the junior teachers attend a course of lectures and take a diocesan examination to qualify for their important work. The teaching in Sunday school is based on the Catechism, and we use the books by R. Lumb, in the various grades that lead up to the pre-confirmation class of 12-year-olds. These children are automatically enrolled in my confirmation class at the age of thirteen. The whole Sunday school course of instruction thus leads up to Confirmation. The children are taught eagerly to look forward to it, and it is a great help to me that the children who come to me have been well grounded in the Catechism. As will be seen later, we find it best to have the Confirmation classes following automatically and naturally as the children move into the right age group, but there is nothing automatic about what follows and Confirmation is, of course, a matter of choice and not direction.

Our Sunday school is good. I never cease to marvel that our teenagers and quite a number of older people, more than thirty of them, gladly and willingly give up their Sunday afternoons after coming on Sunday mornings. They take great trouble with their lessons and make good use of blackboards and visual aids; good order and discipline, coupled with good equipment, make their efforts worth while. Yet it may be that Sunday schools in their present form have had their day. Numbers seem to be falling everywhere. Ours grew rapidly at first, but in the last two years it has declined slightly, and this at a time when the schools are packed to capacity because of the post-war 'bulge.' There are more children of Sunday school age now than there have been for years or are likely to be again for a long time, and yet the attendance declines everywhere on Sunday afternoons as more and more parents take their children out with them.

I would be sorry to see our afternoon Sunday school close down, and we shall certainly not take this drastic step as long as children continue to come. But we have bowed to the inevitable to this extent. The rule for membership of all our youth organizations is now attendance on Sunday mornings only, and not on Sunday afternoons. This change did not lead to any great diminution of numbers because the plain fact is that the children who come on Sunday afternoons do so rather because they like coming than because of parental compulsion. The older ones know that the emphasis on Sunday mornings is on worship and on Sunday afternoons on instruction, and that we like all our children to come to both. But those who come in the mornings only are not left uninstructed because the talk at the children's service is meant to be instructional, and we try to make our addresses at the Family Communion intelligible to the over elevens. The interesting thing is that those who come in the mornings only tend to stick, while those who come in the afternoons only tend to fall away. For this there are two explanations. Those who come only in the afternoons never come into contact with adult religion, and as they grow older they tend to drop what they regard as childhood habits. And they are not members of organizations. Membership has a wonderful effect in keeping the loyalty of boys and girls as they reach the difficult age of puberty. Church attendance, at the least, is a rule of membership to be observed. Incidentally it is worth noting that our Prayer Book knows nothing of instructing children outside the setting of adult worship.

I have said that we are a great church for sports and that we have our own Football, Cricket, Badminton and Tennis Clubs. These have a membership mostly of young people and, like those already mentioned, the rule is attendance at Family Communion on Sunday mornings. The reason for this is quite clear. The Clubs are meant to provide wholesome recreation for our church members and not for the youth of the entire district. They are not meant to be thinly disguised drag nets to pull in the unsuspecting, and those who join know perfectly well what the regulations are and what the purpose is.

It is true that quite a few young men have joined our church simply in order to qualify for the Football Club, just as it is true that quite a few children have joined us just to qualify for membership of our uniformed organizations. This does in part explain the large attendance of children and young people at the Family Communion, and some would not hesitate to claim that it is wrong to bring them there from what may seem to be a not altogether worthy motive. Naturally I do not share that view. Our Lord had something to say about compelling all sorts of unlikely people to attend a certain marriage feast, and there is no evidence for supposing that their motives for coming mattered very much. The important thing is that, having come, they should put on the wedding garment. We try our utmost to provide those who come with the wedding garment of personal decision, and there is no doubt that we often succeed. The leaders of all our clubs and organizations regularly attend every Sunday almost without exception, and the leading figures in all of them are nearly all devoted communicants. It would be extraordinary if we did not find a regular flow of confirmation candidates of excellent quality. We have our disappointments. Some never become really involved or even interested. Some flatly refuse to don the wedding garment, and they just drop away. I was particularly disappointed when a number of Teddy boys started to come to Family Communion in order to qualify for the Football Club and were frozen out. I must say they were a sore trial. They had not got a clue about the meaning of the service and their whispers and chuckles were most distracting. They were briskly ticked off and finally left us, but not until three of them had expressed an interest in confirmation classes. We do want to reach these oddly dressed young men, but it is a nice point how high a price in loss of reverence a congregation should pay in order to keep them.

We also provide lighter activities for our young people. They love to dance. Here dancing used to be regarded as somehow wrong, but I am glad to say that this view is no longer held. If the church does not provide well-run, carefully-planned dances, attended by the right type of people, then our teenagers will very probably go to badly-run, noisy, glittering dances at the less desirable dance halls. The church ought to provide events where boy meets girl because boys and girls are certainly going to meet somewhere, and wise parents like that place to be somewhere where the standards are high. One of the most important decisions their children will have to make is who to marry and well-run dances provide excellent opportunities of meeting members of the opposite sex. There is no rule about church attendance for those who attend our dances, because we must have some things open to all, where casual strangers can come in and have a look at us if they so desire.

We try to make the standard high, and certain special ones are now well established. The New Year's Eve Ball ends at 11.30 p.m. when we all go into the church (lit by candles) for the Watch Night Service; then back to the hall for hot soup and 'Auld Lang Syne.' The Midsummer dance always goes well, with the vicarage lawn adjoining illuminated by fairy lights and refreshments served in the open air, and an effort made to capture the atmosphere of a Cambridge May Week Ball. Refreshments include ice cream sundaes and hot dogs, and careful attention is paid to the flowers and decorations. Why should dances in working-class districts always be third rate? Why should church dances and social functions be squalid and generally unimpressive?

We used never to get any trouble at our dances, but it has to be recorded that in 1959 this happy state of affairs ceased. We began to get seriously disturbed about visits from the local Teddies who started to come along in gangs from the public houses. I printed the following article in the magazine for December 1959, under the title, 'The Snack-Bar Cowboys':

Until this year we have had virtually no trouble with Teddy boys and the roaming gangs have left us alone. This year we have not been so fortunate, and on no less than three occasions we have had gangs here looking for trouble. Once they found it, and both sides suffered casualties. On the others ugly situations were averted by peaceful persuasion. We now take steps to avoid any possibility of trouble, steps that involve the closing of doors and the locking of gates.

What is it that is causing apparently increased numbers of decent young lads to gang up for hooliganism in this way? They spoil the enjoyment of others at cinemas. Their exploits on Guy Fawkes night made the headlines and they have turned what used to be a pleasant evening for the children into a policeman's nightmare. Brutal assaults on innocent bystanders are becoming almost commonplace, and knocking down old-age pensioners, kicking people in the face, insulting girls and beating up children are all apparently considered to be 'a bit of fun.' These gangs consider that smashing up property and wrecking dances and terrifying all and sundry make up a good evening's entertainment.

The parents must take some of the blame. Both father and mother may have full time jobs, and thus may have very little time to devote to their children, and very little patience to help to guide them. Rebellion against authority has a lot to do with it. For years there has been all too little discipline in the schools. But there are other factors that come into it. There is a feeling of insecurity in this nuclear age, and many of these youngsters think it possible that we are on the brink of destruction. We must also remember that the Second World War, with its glorification of violence, is not very far behind us.

There is a further factor to which not nearly enough attention has been paid, and this is the never-ending stream of Westerns that are viewed almost daily by our children on television. From their earliest years our children are fed on this sort of diet. Just look at a typical example of one of these films. The characters wear unusual and rather flashy clothes. The hero is the man who is 'quickest on the draw' and he, with a gang of other people, shoots it out with another gang. In the course of the film you can expect to see doors smashed in, furniture broken up, and a general litter of destruction. The hero will probably reduce a few faces to bloody pulp with his fists, make violent love to a young lady, drink large quantities of hard liquor and kill anything up to a dozen people. In between whiles he will race around the country-side on a galloping horse.

The modern snack-bar cowboy takes his line from these films. He likes to wear unusual and flashy clothes. He rides a noisy motor bike instead of a horse, and carries a knife instead of a gun. He sees himself subconsciously as the type he has come to admire, and he shares with his heroes a love of violence and wholesale destruction.

The snack-bar cowboys have become one of our greatest problems. They go about in large gangs conscious of their power, knowing very well that private citizens dare not stop them. The police cannot be present in strength everywhere, and it is difficult to see where the solution lies. If offenders are fined small amounts no great hardship is involved, because the snack-bar cowboys earn good money. If they are sent to prison, then you merely get louts turned into criminals. The approved schools succeed with many boys, but seem unable to change the worst offenders. Rather reluctantly I find myself coming over to the side of those who hold that corporal punishment must be reintroduced. It seems to me that those who savagely attack the weak and defenceless should be made to realize that pain is unpleasant. A good beating can do a naughty child a power of good, and those who behave like naughty children should be treated accordingly.

Corporal punishment may check the outrages, but it certainly will not solve the problem. It stands out a mile that the churches have a duty here and must not contract out. This goes for us at St. Ambrose's. We must all of us be aware of our responsibility and play our part in guiding the young people of this neighbourhood. In streets around here you will find both the potential Teddy boy and the potential full communicant member of the church. Each boy has to make a personal choice, and we have got to help him to make it.

Our Youth organizations contain come of the finest type of youngsters that you will find anywhere, and I hope parents realize what a debt is owed to those who give up so much of their time every week to produce such good results. Is it known that the leaders of every one of these organizations, with only one exception, is a full communicant member of St. Ambrose's, and is normally present every Sunday at the Family Communion with all the best members of each? The Family Communion is at the very heart of all that we do here, and those of us who have grown to know and love this service realize that it really is a converting agency. It is the centre of everything here and on it everything depends.

The young people of this neighbourhood are invited to make a choice. They can see clearly enough the choice that has to be made, and the first step for those who want to join up with us is to come to the Family Communion. By this means they qualify for membership of a comprehensive range of Youth organizations that cover every age group and all reasonable needs. All members of the congregation are asked to use their best efforts to guide our young people into joining up with us in this way, for this is the high road that leads to full discipleship and loyal church membership. It leads in the opposite direction to that pursued by the snack-bar cowboys.

D*

We have something to offer the children and young people of this district, and this fact is well known. The normal thing for those wishing to join our uniformed organizations or sports clubs is simply to attend Family Communion, and then in the hall afterwards to get in touch with members or leaders if not already in touch. As most new members are brought along by existing members this is sufficiently easy. Some do not wish to join anything. We have plenty of 'unclubbables' who come because they want to come, and we make no effort to get them into anything if they want it that way. Some of these end up in the ringers or in the choir or as servers, but no pressure is brought to bear.

It is not easy to bring our young teenagers into the full worshipping fellowship. The trouble is that odd notions of Christianity still prevail amongst them. What have we done to give so many of them the impression that basically Christianity consists of not doing the things you want to do, and doing a great many things that seem to lack any meaning? Christians, in the view of many of them, are simply people who do not drink or smoke or swear or do anything interesting on Sundays but who like to spend much of their time in singing hymns and listening to sermons. It seems to them that we worship a pale, insipid figure, a gentle Jesus who is meek and mild, whose picture can be seen in stained-glass windows and who seems to attract a largely female following.

What have we done to obliterate the Jesus of history, the man whose presence drew out all that was best in people, the man who by virtue of His tremendous personality quelled a mob of His fellow townsmen who, furious and hysterical, sought to lynch Him? St. Luke tells us that He simply passed through the midst of them and went on His way, thus describing what must surely have been the greatest display of courage and authority and moral stature of all time. What has happened to the Jesus who, single handed, drove the money changers out with the business end of a whip?

We must try to present the strong and vigorous Christ that appeals to all that is virile in young people, and nothing less than this will do.

I am constantly hearing appreciative comments from parents about all that the Church does for their children, and our standing in the locality is high, for this is something that non-churchgoers can see and understand. They see that we really do hold our youngsters at the age when so many drop away, and the odd thing is that many are very thankful that we do. They see growth in character in these young people. They see them doing all sorts of things for the blind and the old and the lonely. What they call 'character' we call 'grace.' The strategy is to bring into the fellowship all that we can and to keep them moving in the right direction. We are trying to win them for Christ, and we use every method we can think of to do so. Positive Central Churchmanship here involves the Evangelical emphasis on personal evangelism and we believe that children and young people can and do respond. It is because of this emphasis that our organizations do not tend to become ends in themselves, which they certainly would if there was no rule about church attendance.

CHAPTER TEN

THE OCCASIONAL OFFICES—PUBLIC BAPTISM

HOW often we are told that the Occasional Offices provide us with a wonderful pastoral opportunity. I must confess that until coming here I had made all too little use of them, and the available figures strongly suggest that something is wrong somewhere. In the report, *Confirmation To-day*, published by the Church Assembly in 1944, it is stated that of every one hundred children born in this country, 67 are baptized in the Church of England, and of these 34 attend Sunday school, 26 are confirmed, and 9 make their communion at Easter. Some really up to date figures are published in the 1959 edition of the *Official Year Book of the Church of England*, and it is interesting to see that the proportions have not altered to any great extent. It is stated that in 1956, of every hundred children born in this country, 66 are baptized in the Church of England, and of these 24 are confirmed, 7 go on the Electoral Roll, and 6 make their communion at Easter. Those attending Sunday school have declined sharply, but undue importance need not be attached to that. It is interesting to see that you still get married in church, and the figures quoted indicate that 49.6 per cent of all marriages still take place in the Church of England, with 30.6 per cent in Registry Offices, 10.4 per cent Other Denominations, and 9.4 per cent Roman Catholic. It is also clear that the great bulk of people are buried with the full rites of the Church of England.

I know the joke about 'Four Wheel Christians' who are wheeled in their perambulators for baptism, come in a taxi to get married, and make their final journey to church in a hearse, and we all of us heartily wish that this sort of nominal church allegiance could be changed into something more active and sincere. But after all the jokes have been made the plain fact emerges that we have our opportunity. People come to us of their own free wills at the most impressionable moments of their lives. Perhaps this is the greatest factor in favour of our Church remaining established. People come to us because they have a right to come, and their coming, often with little or no church background, gives us a chance that is surely uniquely valuable.

Our baptisms here were poor affairs. We used to have them on the first Sunday in the month at 4 p.m., and the attendance would be confined to parents, godparents and friends. There was no indication that the general congregation either knew or cared. We took a lot of trouble, paying evening visits to the homes and explaining everything and inviting the parents to go farther. But few responded.

We decided that something must be done. A Parish Conference was called, and the whole thing gone into thoroughly and a new plan drawn up. We saw that Holy Baptism was a great Gospel sacrament instituted by Christ in one of His last commands. We noted what great events baptisms used to be, held at first only on Easter Eve, then on Whitsunday and Christmas and Epiphany as well, and always in the presence of the whole congregation with great rejoicing. We saw that the clear intention of the Prayer Book was that baptism should take place 'when the most number of people come together,' and that it was for totally unworthy reasons that in Georgian times this requirement was ignored and the custom adopted of having the rite administered in the drawing-rooms of private houses, a custom that led inevitably to the present general degradation of the service into a semi-private affair. We decided unanimously that if membership of the Church is conferred in Holy Baptism by the operation of the Holy Spirit, then membership of the local congregation is conferred as well, and this should be of the greatest interest to all other members of the congregation. We decided that hole-in-the-corner baptisms must cease and a procedure more in accordance with tradition adopted.

It was agreed that baptisms should take place on the Sunday after Epiphany, Easter Day, Whitsunday, Harvest Festival and Dedication Festival (November) at 3.15 p.m. On these days the church would be decorated, the bells would ring, the full choir attend and the whole congregation, children of the Sunday school included, would be strongly urged to attend. The parents would be carefully taught the meaning of it all as before. They would be invited to come to a rehearsal the Sunday before, bringing the godparents with them if possible, and during this rehearsal clear teaching would be given. They would be asked to come to tea in the hall afterwards to meet members of the P.C.C. We would also appoint additional church sponsors, communicant members living in the same street or reasonably near, to help and be friendly.

All this was agreed. The next thing was to get this new procedure generally accepted. I announced in the magazine the findings of the conference:

The Parish Conference spent a good deal of time considering the whole question of the administration of public baptism at St. Ambrose, and there was clearly a general feeling that our present system left much to be desired. What happens at present? You call to see the vicar, who gives you a form. The assistant curate calls to explain everything. You bring baby along on the first Sunday in the month, and he is baptized in the presence of parents, godparents, and a few relatives.

What is wrong with this? It ignores the fact that Holy Baptism is a great Gospel sacrament, as important as Holy Communion. It ignores the Prayer Book order that baptisms should take place 'when the most number of people come together.' It gives the impression that it does not really matter very much to the other members of the St. Ambrose family.

What is going to happen now? We are going to do our best to make Holy Baptism the really big and important event it is meant to be. Baptisms will be held on only five Sunday afternoons in 1957—Sunday, Jan. 6th (Feast of the Epiphany), Sunday, April 21st (Easter Day), Sunday, June 9th (Whitsunday), Sunday, Sept. 29th (Harvest Festival), and Sunday, Nov. 17th (Dedication Festival). In each case the service will be held at 3.15 p.m. with, we hope, bells beforehand, the full choir present, members of the St. Ambrose family present in strength, including the whole Sunday school, and their parents too. We confidently expect the church to be full to capacity on each occasion, and we shall try to make the services as inspiring and impressive as we possibly can.

Parents and godparents will be invited to come to a rehearsal in church the previous Sunday afternoon, and to a tea party afterwards, where they will meet members of the Parochial Church Council. Members of the St. Ambrose family living in the same street as the parents will be asked to call beforehand and get to know them. We want all parents to understand that their baby is being baptized into the family of Jesus Christ and into our own St. Ambrose family, and we want them to know how much we want them, the parents, to join our fellowship. It is unlikely that Christianity will ever mean much to the children unless they do.

The new plan was readily accepted by the congregation and by the parents concerned when it was pointed out that semi-private baptisms had their origins in Georgian snobbery. Snobbery is anathema to working-class folk, in theory at any rate, and this point was more readily understood than the theology of baptism! At any rate there have been few protests, indeed in the past two years I can recall only two couples who flatly refused to take part in the new scheme, and both were for the same reason—'I don't want my baby baptized with a whole lot of others.' They persisted in this attitude in spite of all we could say, and I duly baptized them on a week-day in the old way. There are some with genuine reasons, such as father going off for national service before the next one (or in one case, father going off to prison!), and here again we have to meet their wishes. But I feel that I must stick to the public announcement, 'Baptisms will be held on only five Sunday afternoons next year . . .' and arrange a week-day instead.

The service certainly is dignified and impressive, and here Central Churchmanship is indebted to the Anglo-Catholics for stressing the importance of traditional usage and orderly reverence. Let me describe a typical service.

Mothers and fathers sit in the front seats, with mother holding the baby, and the godparents in the seats behind them. Friends and relations and the church sponsors sit behind them, and then the general congregation. The church is decorated and the bells are ringing, and there is the general atmosphere of a great occasion. The choir comes in in procession, with servers and clergy, and we begin with a hymn. Just before the promises an address is given reminding all present of the meaning of baptism and leading up to a direct appeal to the parents, and then the godparents stand by themselves to make their solemn affirmations.

Then comes the procession to the font. The crucifer leads the way followed by two servers and the clergy, and then the parents in pairs with mother carrying the baby. At the font one server pours in the water and the other lights a taper to light a small candle that will be given to each father after his baby has been baptized. These candles have the date written on them, and the parents are asked to light them on each baptism anniversary until confirmation. Percy Dearmer says that this custom of giving a lighted candle is an old Gallican custom that was general in mediaeval England, and the act is full of the plainest significance. At the font mother hands the baby to father, who hands it to the vicar and names the child, and then receives it back and returns it to the mother.

After the baptism the procession returns to the chancel step where each baby is received into the church. The whole congregation joins in saying, 'We receive this child into the congregation of Christ's flock . . .' and I attach very great importance to this. Our people are taught that at the actual moment of baptism the child is made a member of the great world-wide family of Jesus Christ that we call the Church. But he also has to be welcomed into the local congregation, into the family of St. Ambrose, and this is one of the reasons why they are urged to be present. The actual saying of the words helps to make this plain, and their doing so is something of quite vital importance.

The members of the Liturgical Commission seem to have overlooked the pastoral value of this symbolic action and in their experimental baptism service I am sorry that the reception into the church has been left out, presumably because it is thought to be superfluous. In this they have gone back to 1549 instead of 1552, but it is to be hoped that it will be restored and made less ambiguous by using some such words as, 'We receive this child into this our own church family.' The receiving of the child into the fellowship is surely the great difference between public baptism and private baptism, and we must all rejoice that the intention clearly is to make baptism into the great public occasion that it was always intended to be.

Our drill at the chancel step is that father hands the baby to the priest as before, and afterwards receives a copy of *The Book of My Baptism*, an excellent Mothers' Union publication that is far superior to the usual run of baptism cards. The godparents stand alone for their final promise after it has been made clear to them that their chief responsibility is to pray for their godchildren and encourage them to live in the Christian faith.

It will be noted that the parents play a far more prominent part than usual. At some baptisms it is almost impossible to tell who the mother is, and father is often that quiet chap standing right at the back, who does not appear to be involved in any way. This is surely wrong, and the only other thing that I regret in the otherwise beautiful and inspiring experimental service, is that the parents are still not given a prominent part, or indeed any part at all. They should be given an opportunity of affirming their acceptance of the Christian faith and of accepting their responsibilities.

The parents and nobody else are finally responsible for the religious upbringing of their children, and this responsibility cannot be passed on to godparents or school teachers or clergy. We like to make this clear, insisting that father must play his part as well as mother. The trouble in working-class parishes is that so many fathers see so little of their children, what with overtime both in the evenings and at week-ends to keep him away from home at the only time he could be seeing his children. At least we can, and do, make it clear that father has a vital part to play—and as it has all been carefully rehearsed beforehand there are no worries about father making a fool of himself by doing the wrong thing. The part played by the parents is magnified and that by the godparents diminished, and this is a recognition of the fact that the whole system of godparents has become largely farcical.

The system is working well. An explanatory leaflet is handed to all parents that they can take home and study, and this stresses, amongst points already mentioned, that those living outside the parish with no special connections with us must go to their own parish churches. Those with special connections must get the formal consent of their own parish priest first. I wrote the following in the magazine when the new scheme had become established:

We have now had three of these baptism services and we can look back and draw a few conclusions. At Epiphany there were four fathers and mothers present, and all four fathers and the one mother not confirmed all came to confirmation classes afterwards. At Easter there were no less than seventeen babies baptized. There was a vast congregation and with the bells ringing beforehand, the full choir present and the church magnificently decorated we saw something of the joy and splendour that were always a feature of baptisms in the early church. On Whitsunday the rain poured down and greatly reduced the attendance, but the bells rang out, the choir led the singing, the church again looked magnificent, and some of the comments from the parents and godparents are worth recording: 'I never knew baptism was so important. Surely it is usually tucked away in a corner.' 'What a wonderful and inspiring service.' 'I shall never forget this as long as I live.'

Let's be quite clear why, as some put it, we make so much fuss, or, as others say, we take so much trouble. It is because baptism is a great Gospel sacrament ordained by Christ Himself, because it is equal to Holy Communion for this reason, because in the early centuries Baptism was a great occasion eagerly looked forward to by all. It is because, quite clearly, our Prayer Book intends it to be just that, with an express order that it is to be administered 'when the most number of people come together.' It is because it is a great occasion for the babies, their parents and the St. Ambrose congregation. It is because we are tremendously concerned when new members are added to our number, even very small members. It is because we are given this one opportunity of reaching out to the parents of young children and, please God, starting some of them on the Christian path and adding them to our company. It is because this service is meant to remind 'every man present of his own profession made to God in his baptism' (Prayer Book). This is one of the most important things we are doing here, and I call for the whole-hearted co-operation of every Ambrosian in carrying out what has started so well.

There have been a few—very few—who, after the whole thing has been explained, still want the old way, still want the baptism of their baby to be a little quiet family affair with nobody else present at all outside the immediate circle of relations and friends. Although I know this to be contrary to the Prayer Book intentions yet I cannot and will not turn babies away. I am not prepared to say: 'Either you fit in with the St. Ambrose scheme or we will do nothing for you.' The Prayer Book says baptism is not to be administered 'but upon Sundays and other Holy days,' and accordingly those who, after hearing all that we have to say, still want the old way may come on any Holy day convenient to them and us—and these Holy days are those marked in red in their diaries.

I do not think that anybody who understands what baptism really is will want the old way. In baptism God reaches down to the baby. His Holy Spirit is given to bestow membership of the Church or body of Christ. The baby is born again, born into a great world-wide fellowship. It is also received into a particular congregation. Here these babies become our newest Ambrosians, members of our church family. Some people think we do not care. It is up to us to show them that they are wrong.

The comment I hear most frequently is: 'Fancy doing all this for our baby!' but this is not entirely accurate. It is for the church family, to put all in remembrance of their own baptisms, and to keep before them the importance of it. And it is for the parents. We do everything we possibly can to bring them into our fellowship. Some have been confirmed through this contact, others have started to come to church services, all must surely know a great deal more about the church than they knew before. One of the great things about this sort of baptism service is that it does show those outside the church that the church really does care. We get our opportunity of showing this, and a lot more besides. The attitude of the rigorists who would have us turn away the parents with no church allegiance just leaves me speechless.

CHAPTER ELEVEN

THE OCCASIONAL OFFICES—CHRISTIAN MARRIAGE

THE Occasional Offices provide us with a great opportunity of getting alongside people at the most impressionable moments of their lives. I have heard it said that the most impressionable moments occur on a man's wedding day, at the baptism of his first child, and at his mother's funeral. This may well be true. Of them all, the time when he is most receptive and most likely to accept a challenge to a new way of life is without doubt his wedding day.

Mine is a popular church for weddings, so much so that we have to discourage quite a number who live in other parishes and who have no close connections with us. The attraction is that it is a magnificent church that provides an ideal setting for a marriage—and these things count with the brides! We have nearly fifty marriages annually.

Each couple has to come and see me personally first, and I find that to have a definite time set aside each day when people can count on finding me in is essential. I make it 7 p.m. daily. When they come I first of all find out whether they are entitled to be married here, and then I give them a paper to study and a form to fill in, leaving them alone for ten minutes. Here is the paper:

So you want to get married at St. Ambrose? The first thing to do is to come and see the vicar, any evening at 7 p.m., or by appointment, and talk things over. On no account should you book your reception or anything else until this has been done.

One of you should live in the parish. If neither of you lives in the parish the vicar will try to help you if you have some special point of close connection with St. Ambrose, but the law of the land is clear and must be observed. The usual preliminary is to publish the banns, but if for any reason you want to get married at very short notice a licence must be obtained. All these things can be easily explained in your first interview.

We shall try to make your wedding day one that you will always remember. You are coming to the House of God because you want His blessing on your new life together, and you must understand that this is really the whole point of a church wedding. I hope that you will make a point of coming to some services here before your wedding and asking for God's blessing upon you both.

You should come to see the vicar again about a month before the wedding, when we go through the whole service in order to get the drill entirely clear, and to see what it is all about. It is the bride's privilege to select the music and you should see the organist about this immediately after any Sunday service. They begin at 9.55 a.m. and 6.30 p.m. Practically every marriage at St. Ambrose is accompanied by the organ and usually ten choirboys. The bride may, if she so desires, decorate the chancel screen with extra flowers, and if a large number of guests is expected, consideration might be given to having printed service papers. During the service you should look at each other when you make the promises to each other. There is no objection to a photograph being taken from the back of the church during the service provided that no flash gear is used and that it does not disturb the congregation in any way. A photograph may also be taken during the signing of the registers in the vestry. At least two witnesses are required to sign, one from each side, and both should be over the age of twenty-one. The bridegroom should be the first to kiss the bride. If there is more than one grown-up bridesmaid additional escorts should be provided for them to take part in the wedding procession, of which a photograph may be taken as it proceeds down the aisle. The vicarage garden is available for group photographs after the ceremony, but the best man is asked to make a particular point of seeing that no confetti is thrown in the garden.

You will want to know something about the cost. The church fees amount to £1 8s. 6d., including banns fee, payment to parish clerk and gratuity to verger. The organ costs £2 12s. 6d. and choirboys 2s. each. The bells cost £3 3s. If you wish to hire the large church hall for your reception the cost is £3, and the small hall can be hired for £2. The small hall is suitable only for very small receptions, not more than forty guests. Both halls can be occupied until 9.30 p.m. Wine is allowed for drinking toasts, and we have no objections to bottles of beer. Spirits are not allowed.

The great secret of a successful reception is to make everybody feel at ease. The bride and groom should receive the guests as they come in, and so should the parents.

After the meal the cake should be cut and distributed, and an old friend of the bride should propose the toast of the bride and groom, who should remain seated while it is being drunk. The groom briefly replies, and there need not be any more speeches unless desired. Bride and groom should circulate among their guests separately and have a word with everybody before departing.

I find that most of my fellow clergy do not allow photographs during weddings, and I can quite understand this in a very small dark church because nothing must mar the service. Where the photograph can be taken without anybody in church knowing that it is being taken it is a very different matter. And these photographs are treasured by my people, the one as they kneel at the altar step most of all. It is at least possible that such a reminder of such a moment may one day make all the difference between staying together or parting. Excellent photographs were taken in Westminster Abbey during the marriage of our Queen, and it will be recalled that her Coronation service was televised. I see no objection at all provided that the service is not marred or interrupted in any way.

The filled-in form makes a good introduction for the first interview, and after dealing with practical matters I then try to get to know the people concerned, finding out something about their jobs and home backgrounds and their religious beliefs and practices. It is when we get to these matters that the really vital point of the whole interview begins. Nine out of ten of these couples come from semi-pagan homes, and naturally enough they dropped Sunday school and all church allegiance just as soon as they were allowed to do so, because neither father nor mother appeared to value these things very greatly. Now, after a lapse of perhaps five years or more, they come back for a very special purpose. I get some interesting replies when I ask them why a church wedding rather than the registry office, and the answer almost always amounts to the same thing—a vague feeling that marriage is so solemn and weighty a matter that religion should somehow be brought into it.

Here, at this moment, is the priceless opportunity—and it will not occur again. Without hesitation I always move into action and present the challenge and the appeal. I point out that it is absolutely right to want God's blessing on this great day, but very odd to want it only then. I point out that marriage means the opening of a new chapter, the making of a new start. I tell them that they will probably go on for the rest of their lives as they begin and they must make a choice—are they going to join up with the 10 per cent who are full church members or jog along with the 90 per cent who are not? We talk about the children. How do they mean to bring them up? One of the encouraging things about these wedding interviews is the number of times I am told that the couple do not intend to bring up their children from the point of view of religion as they were brought up—just sent to Sunday school by parents who cared little. Time and again I am told that this is considered to be hypocritical. You either tell your children to do what you do yourself, or you have nothing to say about it at all.

I explain that there is no special merit about just coming to church and invite them to consider the claims of Jesus Christ upon them. If they decide to recognize those claims they should take Christianity seriously, find out more about it, start coming to church with this in view. I issue an invitation to come along to confirmation classes, and the response has been most encouraging. I have so far presented twenty-nine candidates to the bishop for Confirmation who were recruited through marriage interviews, seventeen of them in the past three years, and all of them who still live in the parish have remained faithful. Those who have moved away have been put in touch with their new parish priests.

It is sometimes said that this 'getting at' people who have come to us is somehow not playing the game and is widely resented. It is said that it is wrong and an abuse of one's position to give directional guidance where it is not asked for nor desired. I believe this to be nonsense. If there is any resentment, I can only say that I have never seen any sign of it. These people come to the vicar, not because they have to, but because of their own free will they want a service in church, and as this service is expressly designed for those who accept the Christian way it is surely the obvious time to explain what that way involves. It must be done in love. Only very rarely is it necessary to be blunt and direct. In those cases where the approach is flippant and almost contemptuous, and this is very rare, I do not mince words.

It may be thought that only twenty-nine confirmation candidates out of something like 280 wedding interviews in the past six years is not a very high figure, but I should add that there is much else to encourage. Very many more than that are seen regularly in church on Sundays, and although one longs to bring them farther in, yet it is good to see that at least some impression has been made.

A second interview follows nearer the day, but experience shows that it is the first interview that is all-important for recruiting confirmation candidates. At this second interview the great day is too close for any other considerations to be taken seriously. We go through the service in detail, and I explain the meaning of it all, dealing at length with the various objects of marriage listed in the 1928 Introduction. Couples talk quite freely. I find that the intention of quite 98 per cent of all couples married here is to practice birth control for a period that is usually given as the first two years, the idea being that the wife should continue working and earning. This is the prime motive. A secondary one is that there should be time to get to know each other and enjoy going out together before children come along to complicate matters. I find that these young people know very little about birth control, or 'family planning' as the experts euphemistically prefer to call it. Most of them have read no books about it other than the little Church House publication *The Threshold of Marriage* that I give them, and thus know nothing about the dangers or the moral implications. I explain that three people are involved— husband, wife and God. I do not condemn the practice, but point out that it must spoil things between them, and I add that the coming of a baby should be regarded not as a disaster but as the greatest of blessings. Modern science has done much to help, and I cannot see that birth control, unselfishly used, can be regarded as intrin- sically evil. But it is not always used unselfishly. Young couples so often want everything so quickly. The wife must work for just a further six months to get that washing machine or what have you, and this decision is made time and again and the years go by. This means that the maternal instinct implanted by God has to be suppressed, with risks of severe nervous strain. And the fertility rate declines so sharply after the age of 27 that in some cases there will be no children at all. All this is freely discussed.

We use the 1662 marriage service in full after the Introduction, because it firmly stresses that mutual trust that is so desirable and which the 1928 service so disas- trously weakens. I explain why the woman promises to obey. It means simply that she puts her whole self without reserve into the care of her husband, and if she has any reservations, if, for instance, she supposes that he might make her life a misery by bossing her about, then she would do well to wait a while. I explain why the husband endows his wife with all his worldly goods. He puts everything he has into her care and this is his opportunity of telling the whole congregation that he trusts her as much as she trusts him. Both husband and wife have to be worthy of this trust, and there are many implications here. The 1928 service seems to me to be slick and stream-lined and up-to-date in the worst possible way. 'Do not obey,' it seems to say, 'you might regret it. And on no account endow. Only share. You cannot be too careful.' Of course husband and wife are equal partners, but each has a separate function and this so-called old-fashioned wording appears to me to recognize this. I never have any objections once it has been explained.

Two interviews are not enough, but it is all one can find time for, especially when you add the visit to the home of the bride that we always pay. Even this procedure takes up a very great deal of valuable evening time, but I believe it to be about my most valuable pastoral activity and most rewarding. There is no time for further individual interviews, but a good deal can be done in groups, and outside help of the greatest value is available in most big cities. The Marriage Guidance Council does splendid work in preparing couples for marriage, and three years ago I went to see the local secretary and asked whether it would be possible to give the lectures in my parish to couples who proposed marrying at my church. I was told that this could be arranged, and we now have a series of lectures twice yearly for those who want to come. The six courses we have so far had have been attended by an average of eight couples, and they have been greatly appreciated.

We always have five lectures. The first is called 'Family Relationships' and deals with getting to know each other, making allowances, giving and taking, getting on with the parents-in-law, when the children come, etc. The lecturer is always a woman who is herself happily married and the mother of a family. This lecture is the ice breaker and the chief object is to get those present to talk and break down the barriers of reserve. The second lecture is called 'The Budget' and deals exclusively with money matters, buying a house, insurance policies, hire purchase agreements, a reasonable budget and the general management of affairs. By now the couples know each other, and I find the discussion could easily continue until very late.

The third lecture is all about the sex factor in marriage, given by a doctor. This lecture, illustrated by detailed diagrams and drawings and dealing with the most intimate matters, is not in the least embarrassing to anybody because the lecturer is not at all embarrassed himself. It is most important that young couples should be told the sort of things they are told at this lecture because, as I have said, it is rare to find that anybody present has read much about it. Of the eight couples present at the last lecture all the men and seven out of the eight girls told us that they had not discussed these things with their parents. There are not many questions after this lecture, and this is not surprising, as the audience is a mixed one. The questions follow a week later, when the doctor comes again bringing a woman doctor with him, and she takes the girls by themselves while he deals with the questions raised by the men.

The fifth and final lecture I give myself on the spiritual side of marriage, and we have a general discussion in which I try to put what has been said by others into a spiritual setting, and I put forward the case for Christian discipleship as the greatest factor of all. We go into church then for a full rehearsal of the ceremony, and we end with prayer.

All our couples who have attended these lectures have been thrilled with them. Many friendships are made over the cups of tea and these, I imagine, will continue, but the chief thing is that engaged couples need expert help and guidance and they are more than grateful for it. Time and again I have been thanked not only by the young people but also by their parents, and the interesting thing is that the parents of those I have prepared for Confirmation have been most grateful of all.

We have an annual Marriage Re-Union service here on the Second Sunday after the Epiphany, when the Gospel is most appropriate, and invitations are sent to all those married in the previous year and to those who replied to earlier ones. It is good to see again some who come from quite a distance, and at the reception afterwards I am often told by radiant young matrons that in spite of their earlier intentions there is now a baby— and they would not have it otherwise for all the world!

While we are on this subject of marriage we must think for a few minutes about those whose marriages fail and end in the divorce court, something like 28,000 of them annually. We cannot marry in church either the innocent or the guilty party (if that distinction means anything, which I doubt) while the former party is still living because the service would lack meaning. It is a very different matter to maintain that marriages after divorce are adulterous. Divorce is sinful because it is a clear departrue from the known will of God, and because it weakens family unity, causes untold misery to vast numbers of children, and makes the permanence of marriage that much more difficult to maintain. It is sinful. But so is war. War is sinful for a great many reasons. But just as many of us would say that in some cases war may be the lesser of two evils, so divorce may be.

Only the Roman Catholic Church has attempted to maintain the indissolubility of marriage down the ages, and it has at least eleven grounds for annulling marriages. The Eastern Orthodox Church has always permitted divorces and re-marriage for adultery and certain other causes, and the Lutherans and Methodists and all the dissenting bodies take the same view. The Church of

England at the Reformation denied Roman Catholic doctrine, but tried to maintain Roman Catholic practice and worded the marriage service accordingly. But there is no evidence that divorce and subsequent re-marriage were ever forbidden. Rigorism is a twentieth-century phenomenon in our Church.

Divorce and subsequent re-marriage are sinful, and those who want to continue their church membership must accept some spiritual discipline. But ours is the religion of the second chance. It seems to me to be utterly monstrous to drive them out and forbid them to come to Holy Communion, as though this sacrament was intended as a reward for the sinless rather than a means of grace for the sinners. We have a pastoral duty towards those whose experience of marriage has been tragic in the extreme. It seems to me to stand out a mile that in many cases God does indeed bless a second marriage, and on this whole subject Central Churchmanship is very far removed from Anglo-Catholicism. Every bishop to whom I have referred particular cases has always dealt with them with understanding, and in each case they have been restored to communicant status when desired.

There are very few funerals in my church. Only the faithful church members use the church for this purpose, and around here the custom is to have the whole funeral at the cemetery. The cemetery chapels are not exactly inspiring and the funerals tend to be dreary in the extreme. They provide no sort of evangelistic opportunity. We call at the house when we hear about a death, and it is here that a word and a prayer are appreciated—but times of deep and bitter grief are not the right occasions for much speaking. Practical suggestions are sometimes welcomed, for instance about the disposal of the flowers. What flowers appear at funerals here! The undertakers tell me that it is quite usual to spend £60 on them, massive wreaths, huge crosses, floral gates, empty chairs, and all sorts of surprising things. I have been conducting a minor campaign to change all this, suggesting that superb bunches of flowers wrapped in cellophane might be sent instead, with instructions given that they are to be distributed afterwards to the old-age pensioners living alone whose slender means cannot run to such luxuries. By this means the flowers do not just wither and die, but bring tremendous joy to those whose lives are not infrequently rather drab. We gladly arrange this distribution, and we have been called upon to do so several times lately.

The Churching of Women is the final occasional office, and here it is still customary to be churched. It is a beautiful little service and entirely appropriate. We encourage our mothers to come along for this purpose on Sundays at 9.45 a.m. just before the Family Communion.

CHAPTER TWELVE

CONFIRMATION

BILLY GRAHAM has taught us how vital an evan-gelistic principle it is that we should preach for a decision. His object in all his preaching is to bring people to the point where they want to do something, and in his case this involves walking to the front, there to accept publicly the claims of Christ. The method is not new. In St. Peter's famous sermon, recorded in Acts 2, the preacher is clearly preaching for a decision. Those present are asked to do something. They are asked to come forward for baptism, and Acts 2[38] suggests that it is at least possible that this may have included Con-firmation. They would not have been baptized until some preliminary instruction had been given.

We have to adopt this sort of strategy too. We have to preach for a decision, and the decision we want our interested inquirers to make is quite simply to come to confirmation classes. This involves going farther than an emotional response although it may start as just that. If it ends there the results are more often than not dis-appointing, and even the high-powered spectacular campaigns of such as Billy Graham, leading thousands to just that point, do not ensure ultimate church member-ship. That is the trouble when your preaching has to be undenominational. The people that come our way have mostly been baptized in infancy. We want to lead them on into full membership, and in our church the gateway is Confirmation.

It must be a definite part of the parish strategy to get confirmation candidates, and to get them not only through preaching but also through visiting and through the organizations. It does not go nearly far enough to run clubs and organizations to keep youngsters off the streets, praiseworthy though this may be, nor is it enough to be content with building up diffused good-will for the church. It is wrong to suggest to parents, when they bring their babies to us for baptism, that we are only interested in the babies, and that we propose keeping in touch just to ensure future membership of the Infant Sunday school. It is less than enough to talk to those we prepare for marriage in terms that might be used by any Marriage Guidance Counsellor.

We are constantly seeking out confirmation candidates. Our annual Confirmation takes place in March. Immediately afterwards we begin collecting names for the next series of classes that begin in the following October, and by the time October comes along we have a long list of names of people who have already been approached and whom we think ought to come. With the youth organizations the pressure is brought to bear by the leaders of those organizations, whose duty it is to stress time and again that Confirmation is the normal and natural thing for all who desire to be full members of the Church. They are told that only those who are confirmed may receive Holy Communion and serve on the Parochial Church Council, and it is pointed out that there is a distinction between those fully in and those partly in, between, in fact, those who are confirmed and those who are not. They are told that they ought to come to confirmation classes to find out what it is all about, and it is stressed both by the leaders and by me that nobody commits themselves to anything by coming to the classes. The thing is to get them to come, and thus to have a priceless opportunity of presenting fairly and squarely the claims of Christ. It is then up to them to accept or reject.

The need to come to classes is stressed in sermons, in the magazine, in visiting and at every opportunity. We visit the homes of children we baptize, and the homes of older children, partly to talk about the children, but also, and

E

this is absolutely vital, to get the parents to come to classes. We have a lot to say about the words of the marriage service introduction, 'that children might be brought up in the fear and nurture of the Lord and to the praise of His holy name.' We point out the immense responsibilities resting on the shoulders of parents in this matter, stressing that it cannot be passed on to godparents or school teachers or the vicar or anybody else. We draw a distinction between the minority of faithful church people and the majority of those who pay only lip service, and we lead up to the need to make a choice. Those who show any interest at all, and the proportion is not altogether discouraging, are strongly urged to come to classes. The line is very similar with engaged couples, the parents of the future. With older people we stress the need to make a decision, simply to decide on whose side they want to be. We point out that coming to church has no special merit because people can come from all sorts of motives, and not all of them particularly worthy. The great decision is whether to accept the claims of Jesus Christ or not, and not to remain in a state of in-decision, on the outer edge, and not coming right in. We ask people to get involved, to be the Church, to accept full membership and full responsibility. We tell them that the gateway is Confirmation, and we urge them to come along and find out what it means and what is involved.

It will be seen that by October we have long lists of names of people of all ages, but I must record with sorrow that nothing like all of them, or even half of them, actually come to classes. The excuses offered differ little from those made long ago, and you only have to substitute the garden or allotment for the farm, the car for the yoke of oxen and the family for the wife. They amount to the same thing—lack of any real interest—but this is no reason for not trying. We have ready for them the gift of life. We believe that what we have to offer is of priceless value. There is never any need to feel apologetic, to wonder if we are somehow intruding, when we make use of any and every opportunity for saying something perfectly definite as opposed to vague generalities. All this is simply carrying out the task committed to us when at ordination we were bidden:

. . . and see that you never cease your labour, your care and diligence, until you have done all that lieth in you, according to your bounden duty, to bring all such as are or shall be committed to your charge, unto that agreement in the faith and knowledge of God, and to that ripeness and perfectness of age in Christ, that there be no place left among you, either for error in religion, or for viciousness of life.

It is a tremendous charge. I have very rarely found any resentment when I have attempted to carry it out, but it is not nearly as generally known as it ought to be that there is much very real puzzled bewilderment when we parsons fail to talk about religion, just as much in some cases as if a doctor called and failed to mention the illnesses or disease that occasioned his visit. Never once do I regret having turned the conversation to spiritual things, or led up to the saying of a prayer, but I deeply regret very many occasions when, through timidity or laziness, I have done neither.

The laity come in over this matter. I shall always remember a call on a woman whose husband had tried to murder her and her young children. She struck me as being more than usually intelligent, and I was thus the more surprised when she told me that she was a Jehovah's Witness, and she was bringing up her children in that faith. She explained that she had lived in a street in the parish for more than three years, and although there were keen members of my church living in the same street, yet not one of them had ever asked about her religion or invited her to come with them, and the same was true of keen members of other churches. It was not true of the Jehovah's Witnesses, who, she told me, had given her the impression that it mattered desperately to them where she went to church, and they were able to give the reasons why. My visit led to an immediate switch over, but we cannot visit everybody, and in this case a lay visit, a show of lay interest, would have done the same thing. Our Waywardens and lay folk generally are urged to show that interest and not just to be content with bringing people to church. The object should be to bring them to confirmation classes, calling for them and sitting with them in the early stages. Several useful candidates have been brought in by these means.

It may be objected that this is a very limited and one-sided view to put forward, and indicates a strangely deficient view of what Confirmation really means, stressing it as a gateway to be passed through rather than a gift bestowed, stressing the man-ward rather than the God-ward side. But you cannot explain everything or even the most important things in short preliminary interviews. All that comes later. At this stage the whole point is that people, young and old, should be urged to come to confirmation classes, and this urging can be done by clergy or youth leaders or lay folk; nor does it matter specially what motive brings them.

I take the classes myself, one for children on Sunday afternoons (boys and girls together) and two for adults on successive weekday evenings (men and women together) to meet the needs of overtime workers and those with young families. Then those who cannot come on one evening can come to the same class on the following one. I know the advantages of small, intimate and very personal classes, but these are not possible when you expect a lot of people. Moreover, there are very great advantages in large classes. Shy people are not so diffident. Wives can bring their husbands, girls their fiancés, members of the congregation their neighbours, and can sit with them. The more personal points can equally well be dealt with by visits to the homes during these months, and such visits are of great importance.

Our syllabus is as follows:

1. INTRODUCTION. General introductions to each other. Refer to Prayer Book and Bible and discuss Holy Baptism and Confirmation, showing Biblical authority for both practices and the meaning of each, stressing both the man-ward and God-ward aspects of Confirmation.

2. THE CHURCH OF ENGLAND. Show Film Strip, 'The Anglican Way' (National Society). Most of the adults know little about the Church of England, and many will come from Free Church backgrounds. Statement of historic position of our Church.

3. THE CREED. Belief in God. Is it reasonable to believe? Other world religions.

4. THE CREED. Belief in Jesus Christ. Where Christians part company from two-thirds of the human race. Incarnation and Atonement. Personal religion.

5. THE CREED. The Holy Ghost. The doctrine of the Trinity.

6. THE CREED. The Church. The Communion of Saints. Forgiveness. Sacramental Confession. Life beyond the grave.

7. THE LORD'S PRAYER. General discourse on prayer. The meaning of the Lord's Prayer. Prayer in church.

8. PRAYER. A scheme of prayer for everybody, based on word ACTS. A stands for adoration, C for contrition, T for thanksgiving, and S for supplication. How to say your prayers night and morning at home.

9. THE TEN COMMANDMENTS. The first four. Our duty towards God.

10. THE TEN COMMANDMENTS. The last six. Our duty towards our neighbours.

11. BRASS TACKS SESSION. Summary of foregoing. Definite appeal for decisions. Christians are people who accept certain beliefs and certain responsibilities, and these are heavily underlined. Church attendance every Sunday morning strongly urged for adults if

this not already their practice. After this class a few generally drop out!

12. THE BIBLE. Show Film Strip, 'The Story of our Bible' (Common Ground) and tell the history of the book. Distribute copies of *In His Presence* (Religious Education Press. 2s. 6d.).

13. THE BIBLE. How to read it. The need for daily devotional reading. Distribute copies of the Bible Reading Fellowship introductory notes, *The Armour of Light*.

14. THE PRAYER BOOK. Show Film Strip, 'History of the Prayer Book' (National Society) and tell the story of the book.

15. THE PRAYER BOOK. How to use it. At the end of the class everybody is expected to be able to find any service and any Collect, Epistle, and Gospel.

16. THE CHURCH. The different denominations. The distinctive position of the Church of England. Being the Church. The sponsor scheme explained.

17. ELDERS TAKE CHILDREN'S CLASS. The lay point of view. Leaving school and starting work. What Confirmation meant to me. What Holy Communion means to me.

18. HOLY COMMUNION. The Institution. The meaning of it. Why it is the central act of worship for the great majority of Christians the world over. What happens.

19. HOLY COMMUNION. The service in detail from beginning to end.

20. HOLY COMMUNION. Show Film Strip, 'Holy Communion' (Dawn Trust). Show vessels and linen and vestments and explain. Rehearsal in church of receiving Communion.

21. FINAL CLASS. All come together in church, children and adults and parents and godparents and sponsors. Adult baptism if necessary. Rehearsal of Confirmation ceremony. Devotional preparation.

The classes take about half an hour, and adults are free to go at the conclusion of the talk but, in fact, everybody remains for the discussion. In Class No. 11 I have included 'definite appeal for decisions,' but this decision is whether to continue for Confirmation or not. At many other points an evangelistic appeal is made, indeed, I have come to the conclusion that this appeal is more important than the communication of information. All the emphasis on mere numbers goes. The children have to attend Family Communion every Sunday throughout the classes, and an excuse is required from anybody missing. As the classes continue it is easy to see which children are not really interested, and we very gently drop them out, sending them back to the Senior Sunday school for another year. A few adults drop out as the classes continue, but very few, and our experience is that those who stick a fairly long course of instruction, and who get into the habit of coming on Sunday mornings, are nearly always confirmed.

We find it best to give out the manuals for confirmation candidates in the middle of the classes rather than at the end, at the time when most of them have decided pretty definitely one way or the other. The subject-matter of each class is run off on the duplicator, and copies distributed to all. I interview all the children one by one in my study, and try to deal with any special worries, and I see all the parents. Some of them take very little interest, and their only comment is that they take a dim view of being disturbed on Sunday mornings by their children having to get up to be in time for Family Communion! But most of them are very deeply interested and some come forward themselves the following year. I have a word with them about sex instruction, and find that in most cases there is almost none given, partly because the parents, fathers particularly, just do not know what to say, and partly because it seems to be generally supposed that 'all that' is taught in the schools. As a matter of fact it is not. It is not included in the

syllabus of instruction for the schools of the Bristol
Education Committee, except under the general heading
of biology and hygiene, nor is this very personal subject
suitable for group instruction. I put the responsibility
back where it belongs by giving the parents a copy of
The Facts of Life, by Roger Pilkington (British Medical
Association, 1s.), asking them to read it, and then pass
on to the child and offer to answer any questions they
may care to ask. And I say a bit about the seventh
commandment in Class No. 10.

I think the classes are enjoyed. Everybody likes talking
about religion and finds the subject intensely interesting,
and there need be no worries about making people come
for nearly six months. They make friendships and they
find they know quite a few people when they come to
church. We do our best to make the classes lively and
interesting, and the showing of film strips is a help here.
No pressure of any kind is brought to bear, and each
candidate must make a personal decision for himself or
herself that comes, as far as we can judge, from the heart.
They are told time and again that a full and whole
hearted committal to Jesus Christ is the essential preliminary, that Confirmation provides them with the
opportunities of public affirmation of this, and starts
them on their way with the gift of the Holy Spirit to
strengthen them.

There is a conflict here that cannot easily be resolved.
Ought the main emphasis to be on the man-ward side
or the God-ward? Is it right to stress both at the same
ceremony? There is a lot to be said for the separation of
Confirmation from the ratification of baptismal vows,
and thus avoiding the suggestion that the one somehow
depends on the other. Children might be confirmed at an
earlier age than the present usual one of thirteen, and
admitted to communicant status, thus stressing what God
does, and leaving the public affirmation until a more
mature decision can be arrived at in the light of experience
gained after leaving school. They would publicly promise

to believe the articles of the Christian faith and keep the Commandments only after the obstacles and difficulties had been more clearly seen than is usual at present. Only regular communicants would make these promises and the scandal of wastage would soon die away.

The Church Assembly Report *Confirmation To-day* deals with the points in favour of and against this practice, and concludes that there is no theological objection. The ratification of baptismal vows is apparently an accident of the rite and is not found in the traditional Eastern and Western forms. It was added to ours in 1662, and thus could be omitted and made the essential part of another service of adult acceptance. Such a separation would help pastorally. It would avoid the suggestion that Confirmation is chiefly 'ratifying and confirming' promises made at baptism, and it would enable us to lay fuller stress on the laying on of hands and the gift of the Holy Spirit bestowed for strengthening.

Meanwhile we do our best to stress the double meaning, and it is because this is necessary that I regard thirteen as the minimum age. Nature makes our children into adults at that age or thereabouts, and we ought to be able to help as the children go through the difficult period of puberty. It is young enough in all conscience. The promises made are not always very real. This is why they are so often lightly regarded. I have no hesitation in telling some thirteen-year-olds that they ought to wait another year.

Confirmation Sunday is the greatest day of the whole year, the in-gathering after the year's work from our point of view and the day of decision and acceptance from that of the candidates. It should be a day of great rejoicing for everybody, and we expect and get the biggest congregation of all on this day of days. We like to have the Confirmation on Sunday morning at 9.30 a.m., half an hour earlier than the usual time of service, with the Family Communion following immediately at the usual time and the bishop celebrating. The whole service

E*

takes only ninety minutes or so and this is not beyond their powers of concentration. I would love to include the adult baptism at the beginning, and thus make one complete picture but, reluctantly, this has not been considered possible because of the time factor. We do begin the service though with the promises of the sponsors.

The sponsor idea is based on the Prayer Book rubric stating that, 'It is convenient that everyone shall have a Godfather or Godmother as a witness of their Confirmation.' Very few of our candidates ever have any godparents present, so we ask regular communicants to act as sponsors for each candidate, choosing them about a month before the Confirmation. Candidates are asked to select their own, and we find sponsors for those who cannot manage this, newcomers for instance who know nobody. Sponsors are asked to call for their charges and to come to church with them and sit with them and help them during the service for the three Sundays immediately preceding the Confirmation, to come to the rehearsal and devotional preparation, to sit immediately behind them during the actual service, and to call for them and sit with them for the three Sundays immediately following. A letter from me outlines these duties, stressing example, friendship and care. The sponsors are also expected to bring their candidates into the hall afterwards on each of the seven Sundays and introduce them to other members of the congregation.

At the beginning of the service the bishop calls upon the sponsors, standing alone, to reply 'I will' to the following questions:

1. EXAMPLE. Will you, by your personal example, seek to help the person you are sponsoring to be a faithful soldier and servant of our Lord Jesus Christ?

2. FRIENDSHIP. Will you, by your friendship and encouragement, seek to establish that person in the St. Ambrose family?

3. CARE. Will you use all means open to you to help that person faithfully to keep the solemn promises he or she is about to make?

May the Lord God Almighty give you grace and power to perform the good work that you are endeavouring to do in His name.

Then comes the task of keeping the newly-confirmed in the fellowship, and in spite of all that we can do, in spite of the endeavours of the sponsors, we do have the heartbreak of seeing some drop away. The figures have already been given. The Family Communion does keep most of them and parishes that have this tradition established find much less wastage than others. We find that membership of an organization is a great help, for the rules include weekly attendance. It always strikes me as odd that candidates who appear to enjoy the classes so much, and who say how much they will miss them, yet just will not come to continuation classes. It is vital that they should be trained to live lives of Christian witness and Christian service, and more instruction is needed. Forunately we have this opportunity in the sermon and the Christian year provides us with scope for stressing every possible aspect.

In spite of the setbacks and disappointments the strategy outlined above really works. We have presented more confirmation candidates in the past six years than in the previous twenty years, and they have been of excellent quality. Some of them are already holding key positions in the church (one is vicar's warden) and their devotion and enthusiasm are a constant inspiration. It means much hard work, most of all for the parish priest. It means that much else just cannot be done. But this is absolutely central. Nothing is more important. Everything must lead up to the annual Confirmation, on to the Family Communion, and from there to every department of life.

CHAPTER THIRTEEN

HELPING PEOPLE

MANY of us served as chaplains in the armed forces in wartime. We found that men usually came to us when in trouble, and came to us first. They came without inhibitions. There was never any suggestion that the chaplain might be shocked even by the more startling revelations. They came because they regarded us as their friends, willing to do all in our power to help them if we possibly could. In the Navy the chaplain is supposed to be 'the friend and adviser of all on board,' a splendid phrase used in official regulations, and all try their utmost to be just this. I had seven years in the Navy as a chaplain and I know how much I valued the fact that men in trouble came to me, just dropping in without ceremony to talk the whole thing over. I never had any special training for welfare work but it was assumed, as surely people have a right to assume, that as a parson I was the person who ought to know what advice to give and what action to take, and what facilities were available. My *Crockford's Clerical Directory* was my best ally in these matters. Everybody lived in a parish, and every parish had a parish priest, and I found time and again that a letter to him was the best way of getting immediate and efficient action. What extraordinary cases we had to handle! We became experts in dealing with the welfare problems that beset ordinary folk.

After the war we were demobilized. We were appointed to our parishes. We expected our parishioners to come to us with their troubles, indeed we longed for them to do so. But they did not come. We wanted to be the friend and adviser of all in the parish, we wanted to be true shepherds, we wanted them to know that nothing was too much trouble and that they could come at any time of the night or day and find sympathy and practical help. It was a bitter disillusionment to find that we were almost the last to be consulted. Our doctor friends told us that their surgeries were cluttered up with people who had nothing seriously wrong, who just wanted to talk at length about their private difficulties and worries and problems, and the doctors just had not got the time to spare for that leisurely listening which is the basic requirement of all welfare work. The general feeling seemed to be that a parson was out of touch with ordinary life and lived in a rarefied atmosphere far removed from ordinary folk. He might be shocked as a doctor would not be shocked. Moreover, he just did not know the answers.

I think the last point was probably the strongest in those post-war years. People supposed that we just did not know the answers, that we did not know much about the existing facilities. And they were, of course, quite right. The Welfare State had come into being, with complications and ramifications that we did not understand. I believe this was the strongest reason of all why people did not come to us, far stronger than any ideas that we might be unsympathetic or lack understanding, and this belief was strengthened as a result of an experiment initiated in Cornwall.

It was Mr. John Pearce, secretary of the Council of Social Service for Cornwall, who conceived the idea of collecting together a number of clergy who included a representative from each rural deanery to study the workings of the Welfare State and to meet and confer with the principal officers responsible for working it. Mr. Pearce saw that there was a very real danger that the Church, always previously in the lead in social matters, might be by-passed. He believed that people were not going to the parsonage when in trouble because the clergy lacked that specialized knowledge that had become indispensable. Moreover, he thought that the clergy could

help the various officers because of their unique knowledge of their own people in their own homes. As Karl
Mannheim puts it in *Diagnosis of our Time*: '. . . the
theologian, the philosopher and the sociologist, whose
job it is to think about man and his life in society, can
supplement the work of the Civil Servant and the social
worker, who are accustomed professionally to think in
terms of isolated symptoms and departments.'

The committee, or working party as we preferred to
call ourselves, was duly formed, and I served on it for a
year. Each member was told that his duty would be:

1. To make himself competent and knowledgeable
about the whole field of statutory and voluntary services
within the Diocese and County.

2. To report regularly to his deanery Chapter.

3. To be ready to give any help to any other priest
in his deanery.

We had some most interesting and valuable sessions,
learning a great deal about the welfare services and getting
to know personally the men at the top who could take
necessary action in the more difficult cases we brought
forward, and initiate the various improvements we suggested. They equipped us with the knowledge that we
had previously lacked, and they clearly regarded us as
allies who were as interested in people as they were and
as anxious to help them. They showed us how deeply
we could become involved if we wanted to be.

A Directory was prepared and made available for
everybody interested, and the scheme was soon adopted
by Hampshire, Essex, and various other counties, in each
case with the clergy coming right in. John Pearce has
now prepared a big card showing every conceivable
service and where to apply in the first instance, and these
have been distributed to every church and chapel in
Cornwall, for display either there or in the minister's
study.

I soon found in my Cornish parish that my new knowledge enabled me to help more effectively than before.

Word went around. People did come in the way I wanted them to come, confirming that willingness to help is not enough. Our people may know that we are devoted to them, that we will do anything for them, that whatever they tell us will be in the strictest confidence, yet still in these modern days they will not come to us unless they know that we have the specialized knowledge necessary to help them.

When I came here I made a point of getting to know as many as I could of those engaged in the working of the statutory and voluntary services. I let them know that I was deeply interested, that I wanted their help, that they could count on me to do anything in my power to help them. I found in every case that I was welcomed most warmly, and they made me feel that this tie-up with my parish was exactly what they all wanted. What splendid people these public servants are. Their jobs are often difficult and discouraging, their hours of work long; but their devotion to their work and to the people who need their help is very marked.

The people we should meet in the way described include the officials of the National Assistance Board and the Ministry of Pensions, those responsible for health, housing and education, those whose work is with children, the probation officers and the voluntary workers. I have referred very many cases to the National Assistance Board, always with immediate results and careful and sympathetic handling of the persons concerned. I have found the housing authorities most helpful when I have drawn their attention to particularly deserving cases. People are still astonishingly ignorant of the wonderful facilities available to them at times when help is desperately needed. They still tend to be scared of filling in forms and of authority generally, and a little smoothing of the path is always welcomed.

There is one thing we ought never to do, and that is to dispense casual charity. Tramps and down-and-outs still call from time to time, but it is not to be supposed that

the giving of half a crown is an act of Christian kindness.
It is rather a lazy and ignorant act that may do much
harm if it encourages that person to continue to live a
useless and uncomfortable life sponging on others.
Nobody need live that sort of life now, for everybody
can demand as of right the means to live, and it is only
those who are constitutionally opposed to the idea of
working and washing that prefer to beg. Our aim
should be the complete rehabilitation of the whole person
and a few phone calls can start that dirty and penniless
tramp on the road back to respectability and usefulness.
In one case here we co-operated with the National
Assistance Board in trying to get a young tramp to change
his ways. He was fixed up with new clothes and a new
job, found lodgings in this parish, and introduced to our
Youth Club members. He came to church every Sunday,
joined our Football Club, and became a popular figure—
so much so that he was elected treasurer of the Football
Club. For two years he led a model life. Then he
absconded with the funds, and went back to his old way
of life. But he sent back a weekly contribution to pay
what he regarded as a debt of honour, and although it was
disappointing and discouraging to the National Assistance
Board and to us, yet I refuse to believe that it was effort
wasted.

We have a very clear aim in all our welfare work. We
try not only to remove particular difficulties, to ease
particular hardships. We try to get people to see that the
place to deposit their heaviest burdens is at the foot of the
Cross. Whether people realize this or not when they
come to us, this is the sort of help they most need. I have
had recently three confirmation candidates who came
along originally for help with housing difficulties. When
they see that we care so much they begin to see that the
Church cares, and when they see that religion is inti-
mately concerned with day-to-day affairs they sometimes
respond.

The doctors are also our allies. We parsons have a very real part to play in the work of healing. We visit the sick. We do not do this only to bring comfort and cheer, but also to put them in closer touch with the source of all healing. More and more the part we can play is being recognized. Surely never before was there so much illness of the psychosomatic variety, where bodily disorders are caused by troubles of the mind. It is forgiveness that people like this need most of all, and this is where our ministry of reconciliation comes in. What a pity that sacramental confession should be regarded as dangerously Anglo-Catholic! Confirmation candidates here have been taught from the first about this particular privilege, but I have not said or done much about it until fairly recently because I know the misunderstanding and friction that would have been generated. However, in 1958 I printed all this in the magazine:

Those of you with good memories may recall that our Parochial Church Council spent a good deal of time discussing very thoroughly the report produced by the Bishop of Bristol's Confirmation Commission and the recommendations and findings were published in the October 1957 issue of the *Ambrosian*. The P.C.C. divided into groups for this discussion and came together to agree on the various conclusions.

One of the questions was: 'Do you think, as recommended by the report, that clear and direct teaching about sacramental confession should be given?' The conclusion was: 'Most of the members of one group were opposed to the whole idea of sacramental confession, but the members of the other three groups were of the opinion that this particular privilege should be made available to those who felt they needed it but never pressed upon the general congregation. The vicar was asked to make it known that his 7 p.m. "surgery" daily was intended as much for those in trouble as for those with forms to sign or marriages or baptisms to arrange. He was also asked to make it known what the purpose of confession is, and to make known the fact that facilities are available for those who feel that this is something for them, both candidates for confirmation and others.'

In future the vicar will be in church on Saturdays at 7.45 p.m. to hear confessions and to give spiritual counsel and advice, unless an announcement to the contrary is made.

Now let me explain what all this is about by telling you a story about Dr. Hensley Henson, formerly Bishop of Durham. When he was Vicar of Barking a total stranger called at the vicarage and asked him to hear his confession. But Dr. Henson had been brought up an Evangelical and greatly disliked the whole business of sacramental confession, which he regarded as a Popish practice. Knowing that the practice is commended in the Book of Common Prayer he knew that he could not flatly refuse, but he decided to be as difficult as he possibly could, and he told the man that he would only hear his confession if he went away and returned with a letter from the vicar of his own parish. The man went away, obviously very disappointed. A few days later the police recovered from the river the body of apparently the same man. Dr. Henson never got over a feeling that he was at least partly responsible, and he never again refused to hear a confession.

This whole matter of sacramental confession has become suspect to a good many Evangelicals because of the odd teaching and practices of some Roman Catholics, to whom it does seem to be no more than a sort of spiritual washing machine, to be used repeatedly and with the minimum of effort. Roman Catholics have to go to confession whether they want to or not. The general custom in the Church of England is not to go at all unless you have been brought up in the Anglo-Catholic tradition. This is a pity. It is a pity to condemn out of hand anything simply because the Romans do it. It is a pity to ignore the teachings of the Bible. It is a pity just to ignore the clear intentions of our Book of Common Prayer.

First of all look at the words of Jesus in John 20 [22, 23]: 'And when He had said this, He breathed on them, and saith unto them, Receive ye the Holy Ghost: whose soever sins ye forgive, they are forgiven unto them; whose soever sins ye retain, they are retained.' Then turn to your Prayer Book and look up the ordination of Priests. At the laying on of hands, the moment of ordination, these tremendous words are spoken by the bishop: 'Receive the Holy Ghost for the office and work of a Priest in the Church of God, now committed unto thee by the imposition of our hands. Whose sins thou dost forgive, they are forgiven; and whose sins thou dost retain, they are retained. And be thou a faithful dispenser of the Word of God, and of His Holy Sacraments; In the name of the Father, and of the Son, and of the Holy Ghost. Amen.'

Now glance at the Holy Communion service, at the last paragraph of the first Exhortation printed after the Church Militant prayer. It runs as follows: 'And because it is requisite, that no man should come to the Holy Communion, but with a full trust in God's mercy, and with a quiet conscience; therefore if there be any of you, who by this means cannot quiet his own conscience herein, but requireth further comfort or counsel, let him come to me, or to some other discreet and learned Minister of God's Word, and open his grief; that by the ministry of God's holy Word he may receive the benefit of absolution, together with ghostly counsel and advice, to the quieting of his own conscience, and avoiding of all scruple and doubtfulness.' If you will turn on to the Order for the Visitation of the Sick you will find one of the rubrics says: 'Here shall the sick person be moved to make a special Confession of his sins, if he feels his conscience troubled with any weighty matter. After which Confession, the Priest shall absolve him (if he humbly and heartily desire it) after this sort.'

The intention of the Book of Common Prayer is entirely clear. Jesus Himself absolved sinners, and when He left this earth He commissioned His disciples to do the same. This same commission is given to every ordained priest, and in our Church every member has an absolute right, if his conscience troubles him, to make his confession and to receive spiritual counsel and absolution. The priest is under an obligation never to disclose a word, not even in a court of law.

Nobody in our Church has to go to confession, indeed the great majority never feel any need to do so. We know very well that Jesus died for us to save us from our sins. We can and do make our solemn confession to Him, privately at home and publicly and corporately in church, and we know that if we are truly penitent forgiveness is freely given and the slate wiped clean. We know it. The Bible says so, and our experience confirms it.

None must, all can—but some should. This is the view of our Church. Some definitely should. When I hear of some poor fellow whose worries have been too much for him, and who has taken the easy way out, I think what a pity it was that he did not come along and talk to his vicar and be told about this freely available privilege. Doctors sometimes tell me that people who come to their surgeries with nothing organically wrong, who really want to talk about their worries, would do much better to come to a priest. But this privilege is not only for those in desperate distress or those contemplating suicide. It is freely available for all who care to make use of it.

Whether anybody comes or not I shall be in church on Saturdays from now on at 7.45 p.m. Naturally, I hope some will come. I want all to know that any help I can give will be most freely given, and this particular duty is regarded by most priests as a privilege as well as a responsibility. And I hope you all know me well enough by now to trust me and to understand that this is no new departure.

There has been no misunderstanding and no friction because they now know me. Very soon after this article appeared a person came at the appointed hour in very serious trouble who might not otherwise have come. I feel sure that we must make this a definite part of the help we offer to people, and not only those suffering from psychosomatic diseases, and not only with the object of restoring physical health.

The Church has its own distinctive ministry of healing. The laying on of hands with prayer and the anointing with oil have full New Testament authority, and we are finding that these things have still their ancient power. What a pity they were ever dropped. They are not unusual or exceptional things to be practised only by specialists and experts. They should be a part of our normal pastoral care. I have anointed quite a number of people here, and often something good seems to have resulted. Sometimes it has led to complete restoration of bodily health, sometimes to calm acceptance, sometimes to rekindled faith. The service we use is the one issued by the Guild of St. Raphael, and published in *The Priest's Vade-Mecum* (S.P.C.K.), and it is one of singular beauty. We pray for the sick by name at the Family Communion, thus involving the congregation in something that should be of great concern to everybody. But I believe that anointing should be confined to members of the family and only given after careful instruction and preparation and never widely publicized; otherwise the danger is that it will be thought of as something crudely superstitious.

We can help in cases of matrimonial dispute. Sometimes we are the only people who can help, for it is generally understood that the clergy of the Church of England have the right and the duty to visit parishioners in their homes, whether they are members of the congregation or not. At one time I had eight cases here on my hands of people whose marriages looked like breaking up. There are something like 28,000 divorces annually in this country, and I believe that many of them need never have ended in this way if only the people concerned could have been persuaded to talk to a third party whom both could trust. The great thing in this work is to be a good listener, for it is catharsis, an outlet for their emotions, that these people need. I remember one couple who had had a flaming row came to me together in a state of smouldering fury. I told the man to talk first, and I gave him a quarter of an hour to tell me just what he thought of her. When he had finished it was her turn. I scarcely spoke a word, but they left my study arm in arm.

We must be known as people who love our parishioners and who are prepared to go all the way to help them. Of course we cannot iron out all their troubles. We see terrible things at close quarters, and suffering in the presence of which it seems blasphemous to utter a word. Those in trouble of this kind can at least know that we are praying for them. People here know that when they hear the church bell sounding at 7.30 a.m. and 7.30 p.m.

daily their clergy are praying for them and this we believe to be something of value. We ought to be people who understand because we serve somebody who has been through suffering at its most intense.

CHAPTER FOURTEEN

DIFFICULTIES

EVERY incumbent is inclined to think that his own particular parish is more difficult than any other. I want to make it clear that in listing the particular difficulties that I have to contend with I do not think that this parish is anything like as difficult as many others I know. Incumbents with several churches to look after have problems unknown to me here. Parishes where an amalgamation has taken place, combining churches of different traditions, must present acute difficulties. Some parishes have peoples of differing types and find that the people who come in the mornings rarely meet those who come in the evenings. Some incumbents have magnificent old mediaeval churches to keep up in tiny villages where the population is too small to bear the cost of maintenance. Some have past legacies of unpopular predecessors and general strife and dissension to contend with.

We have none of these things. We have one church and our buildings are reasonably modern and in generally fair order. We have quite big congregations, and thus no marked shortage of money and no absence of people to help run things and share in the general working of the parish. I followed a line of good and faithful incumbents who worked conscientiously to lay sound foundations. They were all Conservative Evangelicals, and I would say that you could not have better people to follow, because they laid all the stress on certain basic things. Central Churchmen can easily add the other basic things from the other side. The rows and fusses were minor affairs and were soon cleared up.

But we do have difficulties that are common to every working-class parish, and nobody is going to get very far in one until they are understood. For instance, I have noticed from time to time a rather touchy attitude, an over-sensitive and defensive reaction to something I have said or done that at times I have found very trying and very puzzling. I have asked myself why this man always seems to be getting upset about something or why that woman can never stand any suggestion of criticism. Now I know the answer. They remember the years between the wars. They had to endure the appalling consequences of unemployment. Millions of our men were unemployed in the 'thirties, and they can never forget the humiliations imposed upon them by the means test. When they reached the age of eighteen they became insurable, and so they were then sacked to make room for younger (and cheaper) hands. If their fathers had jobs they received no dole at all because of the operation of the means test. It did not follow that fathers were in a position to keep their sons supplied with money because wages were in any case very low, and those earning a regular wage knew that dozens of men were waiting to step into their jobs if they agitated for more or were troublesome in any way. My men have told me that for years they had no job, and no prospect of a job. They had no money and very little hope. Some used to go around the streets with buckets and shovels collecting horse droppings to sell to gardeners at 2d. a bucket. Some went from door to door offering to scrub doorsteps or do any odd job in order to raise a few coppers for a smoke. Those who endured these harrowing experiences can never forget. They can never forgive those who, they feel, ought to have shown understanding and given practical help, and yet did nothing to put things right. Fairly or unfairly, they blame the Tory party and the Church of England. The bishops and clergy of those days they suppose to have been comfortable and secure, too well off to have spared much thought for those who had almost nothing. They feel that something could have been done if people had only cared more, and they just cannot understand why it should have taken a war to provide jobs for all.

Those of us who never knew anything of this sort of humiliation and privation must just use our imaginations and ask ourselves what we would have done, and how we would have felt. It was all a good many years ago, but the suspicion and resentment and bitterness are still there, deeply buried it may be, but there for as long as life lasts. They knew want, they saw their wives desperately trying to manage, they saw their children undernourished and compelled to go without. How can people ever forget this sort of thing?

Now they are determined to have what they consider to be a fair slice of the available cake. The moving appeals that come from Whitehall to the trades union leaders to moderate their wage demands, to be content with less, to see that increased pay unsupported by increased production must lead to inflation, are so futile as to be almost funny. My men know quite a bit about increased company dividends and capital appreciation. They see that Members of Parliament regard a £10 a week increase as not unreasonable for themselves. Conscious of the strength of their unions and of their bargaining positions they want more purchasing power and shorter hours of work. They are determined not to be pushed around again. If the whole thing is regarded as a fight, with management as the enemy, is it altogether surprising? It is no use dismissing all this as 'Communism.' My men have no use for Russian ways. It is simply the legacy bequeathed to us from the days of mass unemployment. And nobody is going to get on very well in a working-class parish who does not see all this and understand and make allowances accordingly.

The dread of unemployment is still there, of course, and the television sets and the washing machines do not wholly conceal the lack of a sense of security. This is why in some industries there is so much opposition to the employment of coloured people or refugees or skilled foreigners. Nobody has anything against them, or objects to working with them. The opposition springs from an urge to prevent there being more men than jobs. This is the reason why tradesmen are so fussy about doing certain jobs that come under the heading of another trade. This is why those who work too hard are frowned on and non-strikers are sent to Coventry, and apprentices in certain trades are limited in numbers. It all springs from fear and explains much that seems all rather silly.

This defensive attitude, this bitterness, this basic fear and suspicion, does make our job more difficult and means for the parson great care and patience in his dealings with his people. The suspicion of the clergy is getting less, and the situation is very different now from what it used to be. The clergy are no longer better off than their parishioners. They are known to be for the most part poorly paid, and yet plenty of men with outstanding qualifications come forward for ordination. It is clear that the clergy are not out for what they can get, and have a genuine vocation, and working-class folk are now convinced of the truth of this. It is certainly one reason why we have a better chance of winning these men for Christ than we have had for decades.

There are other difficulties. So many of the children and young people tend to be destructive, and not to respect the property of others, thinking nothing of breaking things. We often find things quite deliberately smashed. When we do, we try to find the culprit and make him pay. No less trying is the habit of leaving mess and litter all over the place, and here their elders are not altogether free from blame. It is the custom here for wedding parties to come from the church to the vicarage lawn for photographs, the setting being ideal for this purpose. We used to find masses of confetti thrown all over the lawn and the empty confetti boxes discarded on the flower beds, but the rule now is that those who make this sort of mess clear it up! Things are improving in the halls. The C.L.B. gave one hall a thorough clean out. Now the members like to see it kept that way. The Cubs are responsible for picking up all the cigarette cartons, sweet wrappings, chip bags and so on dropped around the church. They drop none themselves. The truth is that you are not quite so particular when you live in rather a dingy neighbourhood, but good habits can be taught and we are doing our best to teach them.

Another difficulty is the fact that so many married women go out to work. This is the general practice of those getting married here, and I estimate that quite 98 per cent of those I have prepared for marriage have told me that the intention is that the wife should continue to work for at least two years. It is entirely for the money and not because the job of being a wife and mother seems dull and humdrum after the fun and friendships of the office and factory floor. They would much rather give up work. A group of engaged couples were discussing this question recently, and all eight girls present told us they would infinitely prefer to give up their jobs and settle down to a more normal sort of life if their circumstances permitted it. It is all for the money. If they want a home of their own properly furnished and well equipped with gadgets (and nearly all do) then the girl must carry on working and give up all thoughts of a family for a time. On the whole it seems to work out quite well. They get what they want. But there are difficulties that become more and more apparent as the years go by. These young couples live at such a frantic tempo that there is simply no time for the best things in life. There are some things that must be done before they leave home to go to work. When they come home in the evening there is more to do. Lots of things have to be left until the week-end, and Saturday and Sunday become, not days of rest and recreation, but days of heavy cleaning and washing and ironing. This constant overwork by the girl, and usually by the man as well, this concentration on material things, this thwarting of the maternal instinct, this absence of fun—

all these things make life harder than it is meant to be. All too frequently it leads to separation from church and God is crowded out.

Older married women with young children go out to work too, the idea being to buy the luxuries they long to possess or to give their children the things they never had themselves. It is extraordinary how some of our women manage. They keep their homes neat and clean, they feed and clothe their children and turn them out well, and they do, in addition, a full time job outside. But it is not a good thing, and you see this most markedly where there are young children. These children are sometimes sent to school with the latch key tied around their necks because there will be nobody home when they come out of school and they have to let themselves in. It means that they are playing around the streets and generally running wild when they should be telling mother all that has happened at school. When mother does come home she may well be tired and irritable and unwilling to pause and listen because she has so much work waiting to be done. The things that money can buy are considered to be more valuable than those things which cannot be bought, but which are the right of every child, things like love and care and devoted attention to little things. Something in fact has to go. As with the newly-weds, it means constant overwork and a week-end of catching up. There is no time for family activities or rest or leisure pursuits, certainly no time for God and His Church.

Women working part-time are a very different matter, and this course is open to no objection at all where there are no young children involved. It is possible to get the housework done in a small house by 9 a.m., and a very long day stretches ahead. A large number of our women work part-time in local factories and they are able to manage everything without difficulty and find time to do all sorts of things outside their homes, church work for instance. Incidentally we are likely to see much more of this part-time work for married women. As time goes on apparently the number of men will exceed the number of women in this country, and this means that there will be very few spinsters to do the sort of jobs women have always done, jobs like nursing and teaching and secretarial work. Hours of work will have to be arranged that do not interfere with the running of their homes and the upbringing of their children, if women are to continue to do these things. It has been estimated that 98 per cent of all women will marry in this country in a few years time, and we can then expect part-time work for them to be the normal thing.

It is full-time working for married women that raises the difficulties, and one of these difficulties is that the children are neglected to some extent by the mother being absent when she ought to be at home. Father is away too much as well. My men work far too long hours. Their basic wage is often absurdly low and the only way they can bring home a reasonable wage packet is by volunteering for overtime and Sunday work, the latter being specially popular because the rates are doubled. There is not now as much overtime as there used to be, but the hours are still in many cases so long that something has to go. Often this something is family unity. Some fathers see little of their children. They are too tired when they come home from work to play with them (if they are not already in bed) and even the traditional family week-end goes by the board when father works on Sunday just as on any other day. Sometimes it is health that goes. When middle-aged men die suddenly of heart failure or start stomach ulcers it may well be that these very long hours are the explanation. What is wanted is shorter hours with more packed into them. By way of a start I would like to see double pay for Sunday work done away with. The popularity of Sunday work would speedily wane, with great gains in many directions. I do not doubt that shorter working hours will come as automation continues. Meanwhile the demand for a fair basic wage is entirely right, and should not be resisted; and it ought not to be necessary to make the working of fantastic hours a condition of earning sufficient money to maintain reasonable standards. The present system of long hours raises special difficulties in a working-class parish, for many of the men are tired out, have insufficient time for their families, and insufficient time for spiritual things.

I well remember a certain Fleet Air Arm pilot I served with during the war. His job was flying the reconnaissance plane we carried on board, but he also had to keep normal watches. Sometimes he had the middle watch and had to be on the bridge of the ship from midnight until 4 a.m. Always he was in chapel for the early celebration at 7 a.m., and I never remember his missing. If you care about these things, long hours and lack of sleep do not keep you away, and this is true of both men and women here. Many of the busiest of them and those that work the longest hours are most regular in church and do an immense amount for it. They love doing it, and somehow they manage. But it will be seen that generally it makes the job a bit more difficult.

There is one final difficulty that I mention with some hesitation, but to give a reasonably clear picture it is necessary that it should be stated. Clergy in working-class parishes should expect a certain amount of brusqueness that may be mistaken for downright rudeness at times, coupled with a seeming lack of gratitude or appreciation.

It is thought to be praiseworthy at meetings to speak your mind without inhibition, and to tick off the vicar is a sure way of gaining approbation. To thank him publicly might be misconstrued. Thus Parochial Church Council meetings are not always friendly affairs and there are those who appear to enjoy striking a thoroughly discordant note. One man said to me: 'Our meetings used to be really lively before you came and I have sometimes seen some grand rows! They are a bit dull now by comparison.' I know what he meant, but I will not have rows of any kind if I can help it, particularly at meetings

held in God's name and after the invocation of the Holy
Spirit. I remember taking one man aside after a meeting
where I thought he had been deliberately offensive, and
he seemed utterly astonished that I should have considered him anything other than loyal and co-operative.
'I was only trying to be helpful,' he said.

We do not want 'yes-men' and we do not want effusive
votes of thanks, but a little gratitude and appreciation do
go a long way. I am always thanking others because I
know this to be true, but I never recall being thanked
myself until this year at the Easter Vestry Meeting. I
discovered afterwards that my assistant curate, unknown
to me, had taken steps to line up three men to make sure
that somebody thanked the vicar for a change!

I have used the words 'mistaken' and 'seeming' because
people here and elsewhere are not ungrateful. The
reverse is true, and I have received letters from warm-
hearted people that I shall always treasure. Many of my
people are appreciative and generous and thoughtful—
but always in private. In public there will be this seeming
lack of appreciation and it does partly account for incumbents of working-class parishes becoming a little despon-
dent at times. It may be only a minor one but it is a
difficulty that ought to be mentioned.

CHAPTER FIFTEEN

SPECIAL OCCASIONS

IN the older parishes there are usually certain special occasions that occur annually and that are eagerly looked forward to by everybody. In Cornwall, for instance, 'Feast Sunday' takes precedence over all other festivals, and in many of the parishes in the extreme West of the county a whole week of special rejoicing follows, and has done for hundreds of years. It is really the observance of the Patronal or Dedication Festival. We had another custom in my Cornish parish that was also long established. On a certain Sunday we used to go in procession to the ancient baptistery a mile away for a special service. Some customs are associated with the commemoration of benefactors, some with the observance of the calendar. Lots of the older parishes have them.

We ought to have special occasions in the newer parishes too, occasions that occur annually, that everybody knows about and looks forward to and prepares for. We have been trying here to get certain things well established, and it may be of interest to say something about them.

The Festival of Nine Lessons and Carols is always held on the fourth Sunday in Advent in the evening, and we find that this service, that originated in Truro Cathedral and has been made so well known by King's College, Cambridge, makes an ideal preparation for Christmas. The Christmas Midnight Communion, with the church decorated and illuminated by candles and Christmas trees, is also well established. Some incumbents have trouble here with casual merrymakers disturbing the atmosphere of reverence, but this has never happened to us, one of the few good results of our being in a quiet side street and not right on a busy main road. It is true that a party of four Teddy boys came last Christmas. But they were quiet and reverent throughout, and one made his Communion. On Christmas Day itself a Family Service at 10.30 a.m. is very well attended by children and grown-ups alike, and a feature is a gift procession during which the children lay their gifts at the Crib, to be sent later on to our own missionary in Malaya for distribution amongst his Chinese children. The Watch Night Service is very short, but a big congregation, including those attending the dance, always comes.

On the Sunday after the Epiphany at Evensong we enact the Procession of Kings. After the sermon Mary and Joseph move into position before the altar and the three Kings, one a black man, slowly come forward from the back of the church to lay their offerings at the crib. We borrow the costumes from C.M.S. and the thing that always impresses me is the reverence of those taking part. Careful rehearsal and meticulous timing are essential.

The pattern for Lent has become fixed, and at last Lent really has begun to be observed as a period of special discipline and special effort. People are asked to give up things, and all dances and socials close down from Shrove Tuesday until Easter. They are also asked to do certain extra things, beginning on Ash Wednesday by coming to an evening Family Communion. There is much to be said for these evening celebrations of Holy Communion, as the Roman Catholics are finding, and a lot come who would not do so in the early morning. At the same time I believe our young people should be taught something of the discipline of early rising, and every Tuesday in Lent they are urged to come at 7 a.m. for Holy Communion, with refreshments afterwards. It is good to see them at this early hour, some in their working clothes. Other services take place daily in Lent, but this is the biggest of all. On Mothering Sunday we clip the

F

church, i.e. make a big circle right around it, after the afternoon Family service.

Holy Week gets off to a good start on Palm Sunday morning, and the Palm Procession is most inspiring. I gave out 348 palm crosses this year and the procession goes out of one door, around the church and makes a grand entrance through the great West doors. On Maundy Thursday, at the quiet and simple evening Communion, the altar is brought down into the nave and the celebrant faces the people. Some consider this to be the most moving service of the whole year. On Good Friday we get a very big congregation at the Family Service at 10.30 a.m., with children and grown-ups attending in about equal numbers. Like the Christmas Day service, this is shortened Mattins lasting about forty minutes—quite long enough for younger children. After it the youth organizations go for a ramble, and I know many families go out for the day. We have to be realistic about this. Although it is the most solemn day of the whole year we cannot expect our young people to spend the day in contemplation, and it is good to find that the great bulk of them at least do something to mark the day. Older people are expected to come at 2 p.m. for another service which is deeply moving, consisting of seven Bible readings and hymns.

Easter Day is magnificent, with the church decorated with masses of spring growth brought in by the organizations from the country rambles, and scores of Arum lilies given in memory of the faithful departed, and other flowers. The bells begin at 6 a.m., and as this is the only time in the whole year that they do so, local residents do not complain very much. Communicants are invited to come at 7 a.m., the younger ones particularly, on this one Sunday, because early in the morning is surely absolutely right. But most of my people tell me that they would not miss the Easter Family Communion for anything.

Rogation Sunday was properly observed for the first time two years ago, and we started something that I very much hope will become a firmly established custom. The custom of having an open air procession on this day goes back for centuries, and many a country parish has one now, with visits to corn fields and grass fields, etc. Country folk love the observance of Plough Sunday, Rogation and Lammas. Why should not townspeople have something of the same sort? On Rogation Sunday prayers are offered and God's blessing sought for the crops and farm workers. Why should we not think about factories and factory workers and all the things that concern those who live in parishes like this?

Accordingly, two years ago we had Evensong in the afternoon, and at 6.30 p.m. we gathered in church for an opening prayer, and then set out behind crucifer and choir for our Rogation procession. All organizations paraded with banners and everybody was asked to walk in two's and in silence. We made six halts, and the whole thing took just under the hour. We visited a school, a house, a park, a factory, a shop, and then back to the church. The spokesmen represented the different organizations and the words spoken were as follows:

1. THE PLACES WHERE WE LEARN

1st Spokesman: 'Reverend Sirs, we desire to ask you to ask God's blessing on the schools of this parish and to pray that in them our children may be taught to value and to love fruitful study and sound learning.'

2nd Spokesman: 'And it came to pass, after three days, they found Jesus in the Temple, sitting in the midst of the doctors, both hearing them and asking them questions: and all that heard Him were amazed at His understanding and answers.'

A/Curate: Let us pray. Almighty God, of whose only gift cometh wisdom and understanding, we beseech Thee with Thy gracious favour to behold the schools of this parish, that the confines of knowledge may be ever enlarged and all good learning flourish and abound: bless all who teach and all who learn: and grant that both teachers and scholars in humility of heart may look ever unto Thee, who art the fountain of all wisdom; through Jesus Christ our Lord.

Vicar: May God bless this school and all the schools in this parish. May He bless all that teach in them and all who learn, that they may set His holy will ever before them and so glorify His name. In the name of the Father and of the Son and of the Holy Ghost.

2. THE PLACES WHERE WE LIVE

1st Spokesman: 'Reverend Sirs, we desire you to ask God's blessing on the homes of this parish and to pray that in them the holy law of love may reign.'

2nd Spokesman: 'Behold how good and how pleasant it is for brethren to dwell together in unity.'

A/Curate: Let us pray. O Lord, our heavenly Father, be with us in our homes. Make us to be loving and patient in our own families, forgiving others, as we remember how much we ourselves need to be forgiven. Keep us from all hastiness of temper and all want of thoughtfulness for others in little things. Make us more ready to give than to receive; and grant that in our homes the holy law of love may reign, bringing to us a foretaste of Thy kingdom, where Thy love shall be the everlasting joy of Thy people for ever.

Vicar: May God bless the homes of this parish and all who live in them; may He bless the parents and the children and all who share the life of each home, that there love may prevail and happiness abound. In the Name of the Father and of the Son and of the Holy Ghost.

3. THE PLACES WHERE WE ENJOY RECREATION

1st Spokesman: 'Reverend Sirs, we desire you to ask God's blessing on the playing fields and parks of this parish and to pray that there good sportsmanship may be found and wholesome recreation enjoyed.'

2nd Spokesman: 'Know ye not that they which run in a race run all but one receiveth the prize? So run that ye may obtain. And every one that striveth for the mastery is temperate in all things.'

A/Curate: Almighty God, in whose holy word we learn that our bodies are temples of the Holy Spirit; help us to use our opportunities for games and recreation unselfishly and worthily.

May we learn the best use of free time, that our lives may be enriched by the good and wholesome; and being renewed by leisure hours we may with added strength face boldly the duties and tasks that lie ahead; through Jesus Christ our Lord.

Vicar: May God bless this playing field and park and all such in this parish. May He bless all those who play games in them and all who come for recreation, that our people may enjoy healthy minds and healthy bodies. In the Name of the Father and of the Son and of the Holy Ghost.

4. THE PLACES WHERE WE WORK

1st Spokesman: 'Reverend Sirs, we desire you to ask God's blessing on the factories of this parish and the places where we work and to pray that in them management and labour may co-operate to make the products needed by the people.'

2nd Spokesman: 'If any will not work neither let him eat.'

A/Curate: Let us pray. Prosper our industries, we pray Thee, God most high, that our land may be full with all manner of store, and there be no complaining in our streets; and, as Thy glorious Son our Lord plied tool and trade on earth, so give to all who labour pride in their work, a just reward, and joy both in supplying need and serving Thee, through Jesus Christ our Lord.

Vicar: May God bless the factories of this parish and the places where people work. May He bless those in positions of authority, those who work the machines, those who do the office work, and all who earn their daily bread in them, that each may work as in God's sight. In the Name of the Father and of the Son and of the Holy Ghost.

5. THE PLACES WHERE WE BUY

1st Spokesman: 'Reverend Sirs, we desire you to ask God's blessing on the shops of this parish and to pray for all who serve and all who buy in them.'

2nd Spokesman: 'A false weight is an abomination to the Lord but a just weight is His delight. The integrity of the upright shall guide them.'

A/Curate: Let us pray. O God, who has shown us through the life of Thy Son the dignity of service: look down upon all who serve in our shops; teach us to be courteous and considerate to all who serve us, that they may find joy and honour in their work and may do it in praise of Thee; through Him who came to be the master and servant of us all, Jesus Christ our Lord.

Vicar: May God bless the shops of this parish. May He bless those who serve in them and those who buy, that just dealing and mutual respect and courtesy may add to our common life. In the Name of the Father and of the Son and of the Holy Ghost.

6. THE PLACE WHERE WE WORSHIP

1st Spokesman: 'Reverend Sirs, we desire you to ask God's blessing upon this holy place, and to pray that, gratefully remembering those who built it, we in this age and generation may be worthy stewards of the responsibilities committed to us.'

2nd Spokesman: 'This is none other but the house of God and this is the gate of heaven.'

A/Curate. Let us pray. O God, our heavenly Father, who didst manifest Thy love by sending Thine only begotten Son into the world, that all might live through Him; pour Thy Spirit upon this church and upon all who worship here that, inspired by the example of those who worshipped here in former days, they may worthily offer to Thee their praises and thanksgivings and seek to extend Thy kingdom on earth; through the same thy Son Jesus Christ our Lord.

Vicar: May the blessing of God Almighty rest upon this holy house. Here may each generation enter into the inheritance of the saints of God. In the Name of the Father and of the Son and of the Holy Ghost.

This service went very well, with people joining us as we continued around the parish, and numbers of interested spectators. We sang a hymn between stations. Open air processions of witness are valuable in themselves, and we always have one for the children early in June, when the Sunday school parade with their teachers and as many adults as we can muster. The organizations parade with their banners and colours, and we have a band. The children love it, and again it makes a positive act of witness. Sometimes after Evensong we join forces with the local Nonconformists for an open air service, but I do not know of anybody who has actually been brought into the fellowship by this means. The value lies in the demonstration of unity.

Things become rather quiet as the summer continues. The organizations go away to camp, and the great majority of our people go away for a week or a fortnight by the sea, but thanks to the staggering of holidays there is never any really dead Sunday, and communicants never fall below one hundred at Family Communion. We have the Harvest Festival on the last Sunday in September and that marks the beginning of the winter's work, when we get right back into top gear again. Quite a feature of the evening service is the procession of members of the C.E.M.S., who come from the back of the church during the hymn after the Third Collect bearing offerings, and say these words:

1st Spokesman: 'Reverend Sir, I bring to our parish church this sheaf of corn as a token of our thanksgiving for the corn harvest upon which we depend for bread. We desire you to offer it to Almighty God on our behalf and to pray for His blessing upon all who work on the land.'

2nd Spokesman: 'I bring to our parish church this piece of coal as a token of our thanksgiving for the harvest of the mines, upon which we depend for warmth and light. We desire you to offer it to Almighty God on our behalf and to pray for His blessing upon all who work in the mines.'

3rd Spokesman: 'I bring to our parish church this fish, as a token of our thanksgiving for the harvest of the sea that provides us with food to eat. We desire you to offer it to Almighty God on our behalf and to pray for His blessing upon all fishermen.'

4th Spokesman: 'I bring to our parish church these vegetables as a token of our thanksgiving for the harvest of the allotments that supply many of our homes. We desire you to offer them to Almighty God on our behalf and to pray for His blessing upon all allotment holders.'

5th Spokesman: 'I bring to our parish church this fruit and these flowers as a token of our thanksgiving for the harvest of the gardens that bring joy and fragrance to us all. We desire you to offer them to Almighty God on our behalf and to pray for His blessing upon all gardeners.'

6th Spokesman: 'I bring to our parish church this copy of the Holy Bible that provides us with spiritual food for our souls as a token of our thanksgiving for the greatest gift of all. We desire you to offer it to Almighty God on our behalf and to pray for His blessing upon us all.'

Vicar: 'My brothers, with a cheerful heart I am most ready to do as you desire—

We offer to Thee, O God, this sheaf of corn, this piece of coal, this fish, these vegetables, this fruit, these flowers and this Bible in token of our gratitude and in humble acknowledgement of our dependence upon Thee. All things come of Thee and of Thine own have we given Thee.'

The spokesmen kneel at the Communion rail for the prayers and return to their seats during the next hymn. The following evening we hold our Harvest Home Supper, when two hundred or so sit down in the church hall to a splendid meal served by the catering committee. The gifts brought by the children are all distributed to the old and sick (always vast quantities, and more than enough), and the remainder of the produce is sold after the supper. This supper, an old country custom, provides the answer to the problem of what to do with those huge specially baked loaves that always appear among the decorations! We find the following evening the ideal one for the annual choirboys Feast, when the leftovers are duly enjoyed.

On Remembrance Sunday we make our solemn commemoration of the fallen at 11 a.m., when buglers play the 'Last Post' and wreaths are laid on the War Memorial, and the 'Reveille' sounded. We invite the ministers, choirs, and congregations of the neighbouring chapels to join us after Evensong for a Festival of Music, with each choir singing an anthem and band items and solos, and this is becoming quite an occasion, the only one when the people from the chapels are present with us in strength. Later in the month we hold our Dedication Festival with Family Communion at 7.30 p.m., followed by a buffet supper on the actual date of the consecration

of the church. To this we invite all the clergy of the
deanery and a few members of each congregation, and
also once again the Nonconformist ministers and some
of their people. The clergy who come are expected to
make a short speech during the supper! The following
Sunday is one of great rejoicing.

These evening Family Communions are held on two
other occasions—on Ascension Day and All Saints' Day—
and the result is that people really come and make what
ought to be major church festivals at least fairly major
ones.

I hope some of these special services and customs will
become firmly established. Older parishes have them and
gain greatly thereby, because they stress the links with
the past and deepen family consciousness. After all, we
all have certain family customs in our own homes that
nobody would dream of changing. We look forward to
them and we understand them. Modern parishes ought
to have them too. It's all a part of the strategy.

F*

CHAPTER SIXTEEN

OUTSIDE THE FAMILY

M Y people hear a great deal about 'the family.'
I keep telling them that they are members of the
church family in this place, and try to work out with them
the implications. The great weekly family gathering is
the Family Communion, incomplete unless every member
is present. Members of organizations are enrolled just
before this service because these are family matters.
Members of the family who are sick at home or in hospital
are prayed for by name at this service because this
is a family responsibility. There are many other family
gatherings. When a member gets married then other
members should be present in church, whether invited
guests or not, and should certainly not be content with
appearing outside to look at the bride. Members of the
family should be present at funerals. Joys and sorrows
alike should be shared. Every baptism is a family occasion. If disputes or quarrels of any kind arise—and they
do in most normal families—they should be kept within
the family circle and never aired outside. Thus matters
that reflect no particular credit upon the family, matters
such as inadequate giving or unfriendliness towards
strangers, are never discussed in the parish magazine
because this becomes public property. They are discussed
in private letters that are circulated only to those whose
names are on the Electoral Roll. The congregation
should consist of people who know each other, united
by common bonds of love and mutual regard, and it is
grand to see them greeting old friends and making new
ones at the social gathering that follows the Family
Communion every Sunday. This is our agape or love
feast, the sort of thing mentioned by *St. Jude* (v. 12),

the family social gathering that was such a distinctive part of the practice of the Church for at least the first four centuries. We do everything we possibly can to deepen this family consciousness.

It is possible, however, to overdo it. One danger is that the members may not want to bother very much about those outside the family, may look inwards in fact rather than outwards. It does happen. It does happen that the church family sometimes resembles an exclusive club, with the vicar a sort of private chaplain, with newcomers not welcomed, but frozen out. Sometimes they are made to feel that they have hit an iceberg! There is much less of this sort of thing than there used to be, particularly in parishes where the old entirely separate Mattins and Evensong congregations have come together in a Family Communion. One of the more heartening signs of the times is that our lay people are more conscious than they used to be of their duty to bear faithful witness to others, and to be ready always to give an answer to anybody that asks them a reason for the hope that is in them (1 *Pet.* 3 [15]). They do see that they must always be looking out for new members and must spread the good news. But the danger of narrow exclusiveness is always present when the family emphasis is being constantly pressed.

The other danger is even greater. Members of the family tend not to bother about wider obligations. They should be greatly concerned about the neighbouring parishes in the rural deanery. They are members, and important members, of the diocesan family and should play their part in supporting diocesan affairs. They should face squarely the implications of membership of the world-wide Anglican Communion, and should support by prayer and offerings the work of the Church overseas. They should recognize the fact that members of other Churches who are not Anglicans are yet brothers and sisters in Christ and take an interest at the local level.

They should realize that they are members of the biggest family of all, the whole Church of Christ.

It is difficult to get people to take any interest in the doings of neighbouring parishes, let alone share them, and the plain fact is that there is rarely any sort of joint action between adjoining parishes, less in fact than there is between the parish church and the local dissenting chapel. Who is to blame here? We clergy meet each other at chapter meetings and enjoy the friendship provided, but this atmosphere is often strangely lacking at ruridecanal conferences, which tend to be dreary affairs often sparsely attended. The rural dean is the key figure here, and much is being done by getting together the Sunday school teachers or the members of the Mothers' Union, but it is all too limited. We have initiated one experiment that we hope will do something to break down barriers that never ought to have come into being. We invited last year every incumbent and three members of every other parish in the rural deanery to join us at our weekday Dedication Festival, and to stay for the buffet supper afterwards. We hope to receive similar invitations to patronal or dedication festivals, and if this scheme is generally adopted it will do much to bring us into closer contact with our neighbours. It is not nearly enough for the clergy to be on friendly terms with each other and to exchange pulpits when our people seem to know little and care less about the doings of their neighbours.

There is a general sense of diocesan responsibility, shown by the fact that nearly every parish pays its quota in full. The bishop can speak monthly to every church member by means of the *Diocesan Gazette*, and we see that everybody gets a copy by binding it in with the magazine. The next step is more difficult—getting people to support diocesan functions and to regard them as important family occasions. The cathedral is the natural centre for all such. Our Mothers' Union members love their annual festival there, and they help to crowd the building to the doors. The choir supports the annual Choral Festival in strength and finds it magnificently inspiring. Members of all organizations readily attend things arranged specially for their particular movements, and this is altogether beneficial because it does make for consciousness of membership of a wider family, and does break down any narrow parochialism. It is when we are asked to send along 'some representatives' that the nature of the problem is seen and the lack of real interest in the diocesan family becomes apparent. The same lack of interest attaches to both the ruridecanal conference and the diocesan conference, and we find that there is no great eagerness to be elected as parochial representatives.

It is a pity that these conferences should be regarded as profoundly dull. The trouble, I think, is that the matters discussed and the conclusions reached are not of any great interest to the ordinary man in the pew. I believe the procedure could be improved to meet this difficulty. It ought to be possible to discuss important and up-to-date problems at the Parochial Church Council level, and to forward resolutions for debate at the ruridecanal conference, which in turn would forward further resolutions for discussion at the diocesan conference. In theory, at least, it should be possible for some resolutions to go forward to the highest levels and to be debated at the Church Assembly. There are all sorts of snags about these proposals, but surely they are not insuperable. Nobody can be very happy about the present lack of interest. For one thing, it often means that the Parochial Church Council rarely discusses anything other than the raising of money for church expenses or the state of the buildings, never touching on the wider matters that concern the whole Church. This suggested procedure would change all that because members would know that thoughtful resolutions would go farther and there would be added point and responsibility and urgency. We can learn from others. It is this democratic procedure that makes the annual conference of the Women's

Institutes or the Boilermakers' Union so intensely interesting to the members. The matters debated come up from below. I believe that the Report *Relations between the Anglican and Presbyterian Churches* was widely discussed by individual churches and presbyteries throughout Scotland before coming forward for discussion at the General Assembly, and several of my Scottish friends have expressed astonishment that in English parishes a sermon by the parish priest was thought sufficient! Much could be done to help us to build up consciousness of, and responsibility for, that wider family membership that is so vital.

The odd thing is that it is much easier to get people to regard members of the chapel across the road as brothers and sisters in Christ, and to want to co-operate with them in various ways. Here is a subject about which there is entire agreement amongst my people. People see clearly the harm done by our divisions because they hear so often the jibe from their workmates, 'Look at you Christians. You are all divided. Why aren't you all united?' Here is a live issue about which there is genuine concern, and I find co-operation and friendly relations are welcomed on both sides.

We have a Methodist chapel near at hand, and a City Mission chapel just up the road. We are on excellent terms with both, and one reason for this is that their children and young people cannot join our organizations. This used to be a cause for misunderstanding because when the organizations were open to anybody their children used to join, and quite a few used to change over. Now we make it quite clear that we are not seeking converts, just combining in friendly fellowship. Every week we hold a united Bible study group and prayer meeting, and this is announced every Sunday in both church and chapel. It is true that the attendance is not large, but the fact that all our members know that it is being held does good in itself. Discussion ranges freely in all directions, and we learn much from them, and they,

I hope, from us. They are much better at extempore prayer than we are, but our people now play their part without embarrassment, and this weekly combined activity is very much a part of our normal routine. The City Mission people join us (with their band) from time to time, and we invite both them and the Methodists to our Dedication Festival, and on Remembrance Sunday. They invite us to some of their great occasions and we gladly go.

How much we welcome the steps that have been initiated by the Archbishop of Canterbury to secure greater united and understanding between us all! Meanwhile, at the parochial level, we can work steadily for the building of better relations and more understanding, showing the whole neighbourhood that there is no sort of rivalry between us. Our divisions are a source of weakness and put many off. We can at least show that we regard each other as true disciples of the same Lord and Master.

The new minister of our local Methodist church and myself have worked out a plan that we think ought to be fruitful, and which we hope to implement in the near future. Our church elders are going to meet the Methodist stewards and class leaders for some joint discussions on the following subjects:

1. The points on which we agree.
2. The points on which we differ.
3. The common problems that we share in this locality.
4. Future combined activities.

Meanwhile our men and theirs are studying the interim statement, *Conversations between the Church of England and the Methodist Church*, so that we shall all have a working knowledge of our subject before we start.

It seems to me that mutual study of this kind, Bible study and joining in prayer with our fellow Christians of other denominations can do nothing but good. No effort is made to conceal the differences that exist between us. These differences must be sorted out at a higher level and by competent theologians. For our part, we can see that differences are not glossed over, and we can build up that mutual regard between worshippers and that ardent longing for reunion without which the whole thing must simply remain a dream. Reunion must come sooner or later. Perhaps they and we will have to lose our separate identities in the new and greater Church, following in the footsteps of South India. Perhaps some kind of federation will be the short-term answer. Certainly it seems to me that the old bitterness has gone, the old division of 'church' and 'chapel' is as dead as the dodo. The distinction is now between those who are disciples and those who are not, and it is greatly to be hoped that theologians will take advantage of this new atmosphere and not leave us lagging behind the younger Churches overseas.

Overseas interest in this parish is very considerable, thanks to the work of my predecessors, and there is no difficulty at all about getting people to be proudly conscious of the membership of that great family, the Anglican Communion. We find it best to support only one society, the Church Missionary Society, and experience has shown us that by this means missionary support can be greatly increased. We stick to one society only as a definite part of our strategy, and the torrent of literature from the others gets no farther than me. People used to be asked to keep several missionary boxes going, but in my first year I called in all except the C.M.S. boxes. We worked up to over 100 boxes, which yielded approximately £120 annually, and we raised this figure to about £170 by other efforts. One result of the pledged giving described in a former chapter has been that missionary boxes are no longer needed. Just after the new system of pledged giving commenced the Finance Committee went into the whole thing very carefully, and recommended to the Parochial Church Council that 10 per cent of all pledged should be given to C.M.S. This means that C.M.S. can count on a minimum of £160 annually from us, and this amount ought to be substantially increased by gifts and donations from those who have not signed pledges. We hope to increase this figure as year follows year. We have our own missionary working amongst the Chinese in Malaya, and he keeps us informed about his activities and asks us to pray about particular projects and people. His letters are duplicated and circulated, and we feel that we are specially responsible for one particular piece of work. We collect things for his poorer children, and send them out and we tell him about all our activities. When we had a big parochial mission it was good to know that the whole thing was being supported by the prayers of a Chinese village congregation thousands of miles away. Things like that make the family conscious-ness a living reality.

There is one small thing that we do. Missionaries are not exactly overpaid, and when they come home on fur-lough there is usually little money to spare for the minor luxuries to which they are surely entitled. We have opened a Post Office savings book for our own missionary and we pay in £6 a year. When he next comes home we shall hand this to him for his own personal use.

We try to make our C.M.S. support prayerful and informed and headquarters does much to make this easily possible. A lot of our people take the *Outlook* (the C.M.S. monthly magazine) and the *Discoverer* (the C.M.S. magazine for children) and we make good use of the 'gen. boxes' as C.M.S. call them, boxes filled with every-thing to deepen the knowledge of those interested. We pray for our own missionary by name at every Family Communion, and we muster a good contingent for the annual C.M.S. Rally.

From 1957 until 1959 we had the privilege of welcoming a Nigerian priest as part-time assistant curate. He came to study for his M.A. degree at Bristol University, and he got it without difficulty. He might be called a C.M.S.

end-product, and he soon became very popular with everybody here. He saw to it that our knowledge of the Church in his country was constantly enlarged and to see him celebrating at the Family Communion, with perhaps a few Nigerians in the congregation, was a graphic reminder of this larger fellowship.

Support for only one society makes it possible to deepen the interest and increase the support, and experience has shown that this course is very desirable from many points of view. Certainly there is no difficulty about this family obligation.

CHAPTER SEVENTEEN

LOOKING AROUND

AS I look around my parish I see much to rejoice about, with clear evidence of steady growth resulting from the strategy adopted. The Family Communion, the really public baptisms, the waywardens, the elders, the limiting of membership of virtually everything to church members, the constant search for confirmation candidates, all these things add up to a forward looking and definite Central Churchmanship that can lead to similar progress in those working class parishes that are at present depressingly stationary. There are many such where the incumbents long to see things happening but feel they must not upset anybody by instituting drastic changes. I hope I have shown that people are not upset by these things provided they are fully explained and provided that the congregation is trusted and taken into the confidence of the parish priest, who does not stand on his dignity and firmly maintain his undoubted prerogative. Working-class folk are ready for changes. Their whole way of life has altered in the post-war years, and values have been turned upside down. Their housing, living standards, and outlook have all changed, and for the better. They are not going to dig their toes in over changes in their church tradition as they might have done before the war.

It is true that there are many gaps here, so many that as I look around I see much that makes me exclaim with Rhodes: 'So much to do, so little done.' I am painfully aware of the stark facts. There are whole streets in my parish where scarcely one church family is to be found. Something like three-quarters of my parish population have no church allegiance of any kind. Much more could have been done by me with the factories and with non-church organizations and some things that have been attempted have not been done very well.

Well up on the list of misfires I put Sunday Evensong. I quite expected really big evening congregations to build up, but this has not happened, and we get a fairly steady 100–150 people present now just as we did soon after my arrival. The Parochial Church Council has been against any novel experiment. We tried a once-a-month 'guest' service of a very simple nature that anybody could follow, but there were few guests and less regulars than usual. We tried one experiment of which I had great hopes—having full Choral Evensong at the usual time and ending at the Third Collect, then moving into the hall for the second part of the service. In the hall we had a soloist and some popular hymns, with the sermon preached in a much less formal atmosphere. People were told they could smoke and ask any questions at any point. And those who wanted to do so were welcome to come in for the second part, missing the first part altogether. I had great hopes of this because I believed that total strangers might well come along to something that made few demands and be led on from that point. The experiment was not a success because, although we began with a hundred or so in the hall, the numbers tended to drop rather than to increase, and the regulars did not like this change at all. I could, I suppose, have had a fight to the finish with the Parochial Church Council, and I suppose I could have stood on my rights and claimed that I had full authority to make this change. But this has not been my method. It would have been the finish of much of value, and I felt I had to stand by my undertaking not to make any drastic changes without a general measure of approval from the people whom I regarded as my allies. Thus reluctantly we had to go back to the old ways. The trouble is partly that the teaching of the supreme importance of the Family Communion does mean that for many attendance in the mornings is thought to be enough. And it is the Family Communion that becomes the 'guest' service and the one to which strangers come. That this service is a greater converting agency than Evensong can ever be is certainly true—but I still want people to come to both, and this remains the party line.

Evensong is as bright and lively as we can make it, and it begins with a hymn and not with penitence. Worshippers need time to collect their thoughts, and I am not at all convinced by the argument that no singing should be permitted until after the versicle, 'O Lord, open Thou our lips.' It is necessary to be lifted up into the heights first. Isaiah, in a famous passage, tells us that he saw the Lord high and lifted up and heard the 'Holy, Holy, Holy' of the seraphim before he said 'Woe is me.' This is surely the correct order and we begin Evensong with a hymn of praise.

Another idea misfired that I thought had merit but few others did. I wanted to introduce a system of registering attendance at Family Communion. In spite of the waywardens, in spite of staff vigilance, it is still possible for some of our regulars to be missing for weeks without their absence being noticed, and it is still possible for a young communicant to lapse for a long period without our being aware of the fact. I wanted a board made with metal numbers in little holes that people could push in as they entered. Each communicant would be given a number, and we could tell at a glance who was missing.

The P.C.C. did not like the idea very much because they pictured choirboys gleefully pushing in whole rows of numbers and making the system useless. However, it was decided to try out a temporary compromise for a few months, and we did give out numbers and posted people at the door to keep the registers as people came in. We failed to allow for two factors. The younger ones objected strongly to clocking in for church on Sundays as well as for work on weekdays. The older people never could remember their numbers. The board was thus never made, and after a few months the whole idea was dropped. But it would have answered several problems if it could have been made to work.

I could have done more about the factories, of which there are now ten, large and small, with more going up each year. I could have done more about the local British Legion, a very well-run Boys' Club, the local Army Cadets and the Territorials. The trouble is that there are only so many hours in a day. What ought the order of priorities to be? Quite a lot is expected of us parsons when you come to think of it. First and foremost we are expected to be men of prayer who read our Bibles and study theology. We have to visit our people in their homes and in hospital. We must be well versed in welfare matters, skilled orators, magazine editors, and trained teachers. We must be marriage guidance coun-sellors and youth leaders and appeal organizers. It is helpful to know something about architecture and water courses and drains. What do you put first? And ought we to be people who consistently overwork? To-day the highest praise you can pay anybody is to suggest that he works longer hours than most, but I doubt whether the kingdom of God is really extended most by those persons who are hard at it day and night with never a day off for recreative leisure.

My alarm clock goes off at 6.55 a.m. and I am in church daily at 7.30 a.m. for Mattins. Mattins is followed by meditation and then breakfast, after which the chores come in for attention, the boiler and the grates and so on. I reckon on being in my study from 9 a.m. until 12.30 p.m. working at my desk, in theory at least. On Tuesdays at 9 a.m. we hold our staff meeting, when vicar, assistant curate, and lady worker go through the sick lists and arrange the visiting. Each day my secretary reports at 9.30 a.m. (I have her for five mornings a week now, and how I managed without her I do not know) and takes down the letters and does other clerical work for me. At 10 a.m. the caretaker reports and is given any necessary instructions. On Wednesdays I walk around the church buildings with him, inspecting boiler houses and cloakrooms and everything else. Sometimes there are private Communions or funerals or special services in church. Sometimes there are meetings or callers. But generally speaking it is desk work in the mornings. Lunch is at 12.30 p.m. followed by a rest before going out visiting at 2.30 p.m. We visit from 2.30 p.m. until 5 p.m., again in theory, for again there are meetings and engagements which sometimes interrupt. I am not one of those who regard visiting our people in their homes as out of date and we have ample evidence for believing that visiting leads to churchgoing. We would still visit even if this was not so. It is a part of our job. We often find men on shift work at home with their wives out at work!

From 5 p.m. until 7 p.m. is time off to be spent with the family. I always remember a boy at school who got into serious trouble and was expelled. A master told me that this boy was a parson's son, and I have never forgotten his comment that the boy's father was so busy saving others that he had no time for his own. My children are, I believe, entitled to some of my time, and I see that they get it. At 7 p.m. I hold my evening 'surgery,' when people know that they can come and see me about anything and Evensong follows at 7.30 p.m. After Evensong there are organizations every night in the halls and committee and other meetings and of course evening visiting and appointments with couples getting married. I expect my assistant curate to visit most evenings, and it is for this reason that he must not get involved with running things. I like to be home by 9.30 p.m. Monday is a day off for us all, and I reckon I get about two Mondays out of every three free.

Incidentally, I think it is very important that we should take a day off regularly, and that people should know which day it is. Mervyn Stockwood, when he was vicar of our neighbouring parish of St. Matthew, Moorfields, always took Monday off, and made all members of his

staff, including the church verger, do the same. Everything came to a standstill on Mondays because he felt
that the taking of one day off per week was of such
importance. The amount of work he got through was
simply amazing.

In addition to parochial matters we all have a certain
number of outside commitments, and in my case these
include the chaplaincy of the local Royal Naval Reserve
and service on the Board of Finance, the Bristol Council
of Churches and C.M.S. central committee. Quite frankly
I hesitate to take on many new commitments that would
involve the spending of a great deal of time. We look in
at the various British Legion and Boys' Club and other
activities, but we cannot do much more. I look in at the
factories.

I know that looking in at the factories is nothing like
enough. We hear such a lot nowadays about the vital
importance of bringing religion into the places where
people work, and there is evidence that the clergy are
welcome visitors to the factories and some I know do
excellent work in them. I have always been cordially
welcomed, and I believe it would be possible to get quite
deeply involved. Certainly it would be exciting to get
to know management and shop stewards and workers,
to have meals in the canteen, to find out what the trades
unions are doing and why, to learn to speak the language
of industry and then to do my utmost to give Christian
guidance about the various issues. The need for the latter
is obvious enough. Everybody knows how vital it is that
factory workers should take into their factories their
Christian religion, should work out and accept the
implications of their faith, should meet and have fellowship with their fellow Christians, should form, perhaps,
Christian cells.

It is all a question of method. The vicar can go himself
or he can train his factory workers to tackle these things
for themselves. I have no hesitation in opting for the
latter, and not only because of the time factor. In the

smaller factories the workers go there to work, and when
it is time to knock off they go home. What would they
make of a parson walking around in working hours?
The workers might think him to be the boss's man,
engaged by him to boost production or suppress grievances. The boss, on the other hand, might think him
something of a nuisance if he stops to talk to men who
are supposed to be working. The taking of services in
the canteen during the dinner hour is of questionable
value.

I believe the main objects can be achieved and should
be achieved by convinced Christians working in the
factories. They are the Anglican priest-workers, and it is
here that the priesthood of the laity comes in. By this
term I simply mean that the laity are perfectly capable of
offering to God the worship that belongs to him and
including in that offering all that they have and all that
they do. Properly trained, they can do in the factories
all the things we want to see done. They can get themselves elected to office in their trades unions, they can
become shop stewards, they can bring Christian principles
to bear, they can bear faithful witness, they can encourage
young apprentices to remain steadfast in a hostile atmosphere, they can do these things in a way that factory-
visiting parsons just cannot do. But they must be trained
to do these things. They all live in parishes, and the
people I have in mind are probably pillars of their
parish churches. We must train them, and it is here
that we need help from specialist factory chaplains who
really know what they are talking about. We are not
getting enough at present. Every industrial diocese ought
to have one or more specialist priests who not only do the
vitally important job of going into the factories, but who
also regard it as of prime importance that their knowledge
should be imparted to the incumbents of the parishes
where the men live. They should help us to train the men
who are actually going to do the job. It is here that the
Church of England Men's Society could do so much. This

great society could be the spearhead if all the members would undertake this special responsibility, and their distinctive badge could soon symbolize the Church in action.

Training men and women for work of this kind in the factories and training them for evangelism generally—here is something that really is of the first importance. Anything that helps people to understand their faith better is of value, and it is for this reason that I want to extend the idea of house meetings. We have had quite a lot of these, some taken by us and some by Church Army experts in this sort of work. The plan is that somebody in a street, preferably the Waywarden, should invite both the known Christians and those that seem likely to be interested to a friendly meeting to hear what the Church is all about, and to discuss freely any points that may arise. House meetings are of great value for several reasons, one being the bringing of the Gospel into the homes of the parish, and another the extending of hospitality and friendship towards neighbours. Although a few new people have been brought into our fellowship through these meetings, I believe the chief good has been amongst the regulars themselves. Each meeting ends with prayer.

I do not think these meetings will grow into House Communions. Our whole Church owes a great debt to Canon Southcott for initiating his great experiment and showing us what great things can be done in the actual houses by celebrations of Holy Communion on the kitchen table, with friends and neighbours gathered around. I can well believe that for many the whole service is filled with deep meaning and the idea of bringing the Gospel into the home is something that is absolutely right. It stresses 'being the Church' as opposed to 'coming to church.' I have a reason for not holding them here except for the sick who cannot come. The reason is that there is one great danger attached to the whole Family Communion movement, one I have already mentioned, and that is a general cheapening of discipline and preparation. You have to watch that in a parish where regular weekly Communion is a comparatively recent innovation. I do not urge my people generally to come more than once a week, and am not in the least disturbed that comparatively few come to the weekday celebrations. St. Paul was very disturbed about the Corinthian communicants, so much so that he said:

Wherefore whosoever shall eat this bread, and drink this cup of the Lord, unworthily, shall be guilty of the body and blood of the Lord. But let a man examine himself, and so let him eat of that bread, and drink of that cup. For he that eateth and drinketh unworthily, eateth and drinketh damnation to himself, not discerning the Lord's body. (1 *Cor.* 11[27-29])

In a parish where there has been a long tradition of regular, well-prepared acts of Communion it would, of course, be different, but I do not think it would do here. If my people come Sunday by Sunday after due preparation this is asking a very great deal and, accordingly, celebrations of Holy Communion must be confined to the parish church.

I do not worry about fairly small numbers at weekday celebrations of Holy Communion, but we do try to have them at times people can come. There is one every Wednesday at 10.30 a.m., which is meant for the elderly; and one on Fridays at 10.45 a.m., which is drastically shortened to about ten minutes and is meant for mothers with prams and small children. We do not mind any amount of noise at this service! On Red Letter Saints' days we have an evening celebration at 7 p.m. with a short address and a hymn, and anything up to about 30 come. In Lent we urge our young people to come every Tuesday at 7 a.m., and we usually work up to about 50. But our regular early morning celebrations are very thinly attended. Once a week is probably enough for most of our people.

We owe a great deal to these pioneers, Canon South-cott, Mervyn Stockwood and others; whether we agree with all that they say or do is really immaterial. We owe a great deal because they make us think out our whole parish strategy and bring before us some vital aspect that we have perhaps neglected. They make a positive contribution. I have much less use for the prophets of doom, those who like telling us that our Church is out of touch with the man in the street, that our system is all wrong, our services dead as mutton, and our Prayer Book out of date. It is so easy to denigrate, so much more difficult to be positive.

Those who do the running down usually have in mind the working classes, parishioners such as mine. I hope I have said enough to show that what they say is just not true. The Church of England can speak to the working classes in a language they can understand, and where results are disappointing it is not because of the system, nor is it because of the Prayer Book. Of course, Prayer Book revision will have to come, if only to avoid the present wide diversity of use which causes such confusion when people move to a new parish. But I hope the revision will not be too drastic because I have a feeling that it is a new strategy rather than a new book which is going to lead to more encouraging spiritual results.

I have an unshakeable faith in the Church of England, catholic and reformed. We maintain all the essentials of faith and order and we are a true part of the visible One, Holy, Catholic, and Apostolic Church founded by Christ Himself. We are a bridge-church and we are in a unique position to contribute much to the reunited Church, which, under God, will surely come. Meanwhile there is no need for panic measures and drastic changes. If the concern is really with the working classes and if the general feeling is that they ought to be our chief responsibility, then for goodness' sake let us give them that Central Churchmanship that combines the best features of our existing traditions and not seek for something new. The Prayer Book, properly used, is reasonably adequate and only minor alterations, such as the elimination of archaisms, are needed to bring it very much up to date.

The parochial system is not out of date either. We have a very great advantage over all other Churches by having the spiritual oversight of a definite area instead of merely a congregation, and this fact is recognized and valued, as witness the outcry, and not only from churchgoers, when a parish is threatened with suppression or amalgamation. But we have to be realistic. The number of men ordained annually is just over 500, and the number of deaths and retirements is just about 600. Manning the existing parishes is going to become more and more difficult, and amalgamations, however unwelcome, will have to be accepted, and this at a time when the Church of England is beginning to appeal to a class of people who for years have had little use for it. Older men will have to come forward for ordination as a stop-gap measure if efficiency is to be maintained. There must be many men who retire, with years of active life ahead of them and years of faithful lay service behind them, who would accept ordination for the definite task of helping with priestly functions, i.e. celebrating Holy Communion, solemnizing weddings, blessing and absolving—and perhaps nothing else. They need not preach nor become involved in the many matters that younger men naturally expect to undertake, because they would not have the physical strength nor perhaps the ability to do so. They would never seek independent charges. Given a couple of such elderly assistants I could cope with another parish in addition to my own, even if the coping would be only a holding action.

Only a holding action is required. I expect to see, in the years ahead, a growing number of enthusiastic working-class youngsters offering themselves for ordination, youngsters moreover of sound educational backgrounds, products of our state grammar or comprehensive schools whose ability has taken them to the university. There is no need for depression. The future is bright with hope.

It is bright with hope just because God reigns. GOD REIGNS! Those words should be writ large at the back of our minds, and they should control all our planning and thinking. It is possible to hold up the good purposes of Almighty God but never to defeat them and the sober truth is that, in spite of all our failings and divisions, God must prevail. Tides go out but they always come in again.

I have tried to tell the story a working-class parish that is seeking the Way and where the tide is on the turn. A strategy that is conceived in prayer and carried out in love is bound to bring the definite results that we all long to see.